For too many—and fo
as it has been absent.
by its own mysterious
our perspective and ou

The very title of this book, *The Art of Joy*, changes our paradigm, for joy is indeed an art! Once understood, joy becomes predictable and abiding.

Tracey is a friend, peer, and someone I've often had the privilege of mentoring. (Though I always learn equally from him as he claims he learns from me.)

As chairman of Champion Network of Pastors with Joel Osteen/Lakewood Church, I have the honor to pastor pastors. Tracey Armstrong represents a new breed of pastors who are leading what's been called "the hope movement"! Tracey is a gift to the whole body of Christ. He carries a powerful prophetic voice to the nations and generations—and has the virtue to match the gift. Sharing three key principles based upon the life of Old Testament matriarch Sarah, along with ancient applicable wisdom of King David, Tracey will help you come to know and grow in *The Art of Joy*. Enjoy.

—Phil Munsey
Chairman, Champion Network of Pastors
Joel Osteen Ministries/Lakewood Church

I met Tracey Armstrong seven years ago during our first Healing Explosion conference in Seattle, Washington. He was an excellent speaker who ministered healing in the grace and joy of the Lord. Our hearts were instantly bonded together as we served side by side in Papa's rich atmosphere of joy and love.

In his book *The Art of Joy* Tracey displays a transparency of heart that brings both courage and strength to the reader. Even in the midst of personal trials, when a believer sees that he is co-seated in heavenly places with Christ Jesus then everything changes. The joy of heaven trumps circumstances, sustaining the beloved child of God with supernatural energy, faith, and the perspective of an overcomer.

As you read every page, you can follow Tracey on his journey where you will discover the divine mystery of how to live in the "fullness of joy" spoken of in Psalm 16:11: "In your presence there is fullness of joy; at your right hand are pleasures forevermore" (ESV). The joy of the Lord will strengthen you to fulfill your destiny!

—Georgian Banov
General director, The Bulgarian Bible Project
President and cofounder, Global Celebration and
Global Celebration School of Supernatural Ministry

The psalmist stated in Psalm 16:11 that in God's presence is fullness of joy! This is a key to life. We must find His presence! In the book *The Art of Joy* you will find the keys to freedom. Every word written by my friend Pastor Tracey Armstrong will push you to begin to confront the disappointment, hurts, and confusion that lie in the depths of a heart God so deeply desires to heal.

There should be a message on the front of the book that states: "WARNING! Contents of this message may be harmful to your old mind-set!" This book is real, refreshing, and raw! It will remind you that God has greater days planned for your future, and that you are called to be an overcomer and victor.

I was personally touched in a profound way by this book. Oftentimes it is those with the loudest voice, highest profile, and seemingly strongest platform who need the greatest inner healing. This timely, God-breathed message of hope is a must for every person who is ready to walk in victory, hope, and authority. This book is destined to be one of the greatest books written in a generation and a classic for generations to come! This book should be in the library of every leader, on desk of every CEO, and on the coffee table of every home. Get this book! You deserve it!

—Pat Schatzline
President, Remnant Ministries International
Author, *Why Is God So Mad at Me?*,
I Am Remnant, and *Unqualified*

Having known Tracey for many years, I've grown in great respect for the man. *The Art of Joy* is a gift to you from someone who has spent years mastering what's written on these pages. You are not just about to read a book, you're about to get to know the man Tracey Armstrong and his God. I know your life is about to change. Mine has!

—PAUL BRADY
SENIOR PASTOR, LIVING RIVERS EUROPE AND USA

THE

ART

OF

J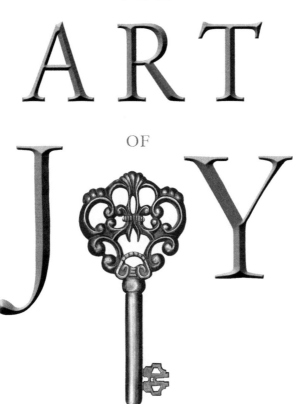Y

TRACEY ARMSTRONG

CHARISMA
HOUSE

Cover design by Lisa Rae McClure
Design Director: Justin Evans

Visit the author's website at www.traceyarmstrong.com.

Library of Congress Cataloging-in-Publication Data:
Armstrong, Tracey.
  The art of joy / by Tracey Armstrong.
     pages cm
  Includes bibliographical references.
  ISBN 978-1-62136-653-9 (trade paper) -- ISBN 978-1-62136-654-6
(e-book)
  1. Suffering--Religious aspects--Christianity. 2. Disappointment--
Religious aspects--Christianity. I. Title.
  BV4909.A76 2015
  248.8'6--dc23
                                    2014049550

First edition

15 16 17 18 19 — 987654321
Printed in the United States of America

This book is dedicated to those of you who wake up each day disappointed and frustrated with life. It is dedicated to you who have lost your way and are shipwrecked in your faith, and to those who are hurting because of tragic loss and devastating circumstances and now believe that God has forsaken them. This book is dedicated to the next generation—may your hope in God return to you and your faith for the future become strong again. Finally, this book is for anyone who treasures a life of joy.

CONTENTS

PART III:
LIVING IN GOD'S GOODNESS NOW

ACKNOWLEDGMENTS

I acknowledge and thank my best friend and spouse, Nathalie Armstrong, who survived living with a disappointed person and never lost her faith and ability to encourage.

I would like to acknowledge my wonderful children, Tristen, Yosef, and Sophia who are amazing at believing and forgiving. I learn so much from you every day.

Special thanks to Kim Kralman, who spent hours reading and editing the manuscript and encouraging me that it is a worthwhile work.

Thanks also to the best staff and ministry team, who always serve God with excellence.

And I am especially thankful for Oral Roberts, who brought us the message that God is a good God.

INTRODUCTION

Years ago my wife, Nathalie, and I moved from San Diego to Seattle, where we took over a faltering church in a challenged neighborhood. The church was dying, and many of the people lived in poverty. I felt that my training as a success and results coach would empower me to impact the area and its people, but I soon realized that my insight and instruction would not be enough. My "you can" would not supersede their "I can't." It doesn't matter how much others want a better life or how much you want it for them. They can only benefit from your strength when their disappointments are healed and they find an "I can" of their own.

Our approach to life is rooted in past experiences that can dictate our future outcomes by governing our decisions and determining how we deal with our responsibilities. The "I can't" road never leads to God's best. The purpose of this book is to help us recognize that road for what it is and find the strength to change course. We can't do it with positive-thinking exercises or other people's encouragement. What we need is to get at the root of the issue.

This book began with an early-morning prompting from the Holy Spirit. I had just awakened for prayer when He whispered, "Write a book on disappointment."

His words surprised me because I had already written an outline for a book on an entirely different topic. In obedience I set my heart to write *this book*. My approach is different from any writing I have done in the past. I don't have a degree in psychology or any behavioral science. Nor did I find the topic particularly relevant to my life. I had no sense of struggling with disappointment. I was happy and life was moving along nicely! My family was great; my ministry and church were finding their rhythm. My business was progressing more slowly than I desired, but I didn't feel disappointed about it.

So why was I directed to write a book about disappointment?

After just a few weeks of research my issues with past disappointments were exposed. Although I had not maintained feelings of disappointment, its effects were impacting my current decision-making abilities. The more research I did, the more my eyes were opened to an important fact: even in the absence of feelings related to disappointment, I acted out my disappointment in total unawareness! Internal voices urged me to reason away opportunities that came my way. These promptings came from the voice of disappointment!

Looking back over my life with fresh eyes, I remembered a time when I lived in disappointment and asked God tough questions: "Why didn't You...? How come You...?" Regardless of how you answer these, my questions revealed an accusatory posture toward God. When He did something for someone else, my first reaction was not to rejoice in His goodness, but to laugh. I did it almost cynically because I did not *personally* know God to be good in my life. I believed that He did good things, just not for me.

Although I could not understand it, I sensed unfairness. The belief that God was only good to some people some of the time began to firm up inside me, even as I preached each week about trusting Him. Always I left the pulpit wondering about God and even doubting His intentions toward me. When I prayed and saw miracles in other people's lives, I wondered, "Why doesn't this happen for me?"

Now I understand that over time experiences and circumstances had diminished God's image in my mind. The jealousy I felt when others achieved their dreams was an echo from my past. It showed that my life had been dramatically affected by disappointments dating back to my childhood.

Could this be your story too? Maybe you have never thought of God as being particularly good or bad. Or perhaps you have been well conditioned to the statement, "God is good!" and the response, "All the time!" These statements can easily become clichés without sincerity or meaning.

At some point they did for me. There was an awkward feeling deep inside about God *always* being good. It seemed as if people who said He was did not really mean it. I cannot speak for anyone else, but I know this much: unless we deal with our disappointment, our claims that God is good will eventually ring hollow.

THE VOICE OF DISAPPOINTMENT

Disappointed people fall into two categories. Members of the first group recognize that they have been disappointed by life, people, God, or themselves. Often they wear their feelings on their sleeves. The second group can be harder to detect. Its members are self-deceived. They don't want to recognize their true state of disappointment, so they set it aside and carry on as though nothing were wrong. Unfortunately people in both groups suffer the subtractive effects of disappointment.

I was in the second category. The more I pondered the cause and effect of disappointment, the more I realized that I had not escaped any of it. Instead, I had experienced enough disappointment in life to become accustomed to things going wrong. In all honesty I would attribute some of my negative circumstances to my own destructive tendencies and self-sabotage, both of which were based in the internal voice of disappointment.

That voice is not prejudiced. Whether your disappointment began with a tragic event such as a loved one's fatal accident or came (as mine did) from many small events and failures, the voice of disappointment will eventually make way for a *relationship with disappointment.* However small or great, disappointment's voice will dictate how you live—if you let it.

The topic was bigger than I first understood. The more I prayed about what to write and the more reading I did on the subject, the more I realized that disappointment had been my lifelong companion. My first reaction to this revelation was interesting: instead of immediately deciding that it was time to get healthy, I found myself making excuses and finding ways to blame someone else.

Yes, I became a victim in my mind.

My inner voice became prominent. It agreed with the voice of disappointment, saying, "No one understands! No one cares! Things never go my way!"

What I didn't understand was that the voice of disappointment does not like singing alone. For it to have power, an additional voice must agree with it. It needed my inner voice to line up, and it needed reference points from my past to confirm my victimization. Then disappointment would fully control my emotions, leading to discouragement, depression, or worse.

When you are disappointed, you feel stuck. I know. I have been there and wondered, "What have I done wrong? Why do I deserve such pain and frustration? Why are other people excelling while I seem to be standing still?"

This is how disappointment talks. My research exposed its language and forced to the surface feelings that I had pushed down in order to function. We all do this to some degree at one time or another; but ignoring or moving past the issue without confronting it means the original wound will not be healed.

Often the underlying events are commonplace; not all of them involve disappointment per se. Whatever the occurrence or level of trauma, past events affect future experiences. At an early age my wife was bitten by a very large rottweiler. The dog was aggressive and attacked fiercely. Although Nathalie has been physically and emotionally healed, her awareness of large dogs is still heightened. When she sees one, she has to address the caution that arises within her.

Disappointment works the same way. It is both a feeling and a reaction to something unfortunate about which we cannot make sense. Simply moving past the issue does not resolve it. If a new, hard-to-process event occurs, it finds the old wound and reopens it. This is exactly what happened to me.

OUT FROM HIDING

The reason I had been chosen by God to write on this subject became crystal clear: I was still bound by the effects of disappointment. Every decision I made was tainted by past experiences that brought voices into the decision-making process. I am not talking about learning well from experience; I am talking about what science calls *scotomas*—blind spots. Mine hid the effects of disappointment. It was as though my thinking were covered over with scar tissue that kept me from acting effectively and imposed limits around me.

Another realization surfaced: I had hidden my disappointment under pride, which manifested as jealousy. Of course, I rationalized this as a healthy sense of competition. When self-pity showed up I justified it too. "After all," I told myself, "I am just as talented as they are. Life just isn't fair, and God doesn't really care!" Of course, I could not let anyone know how I felt or what I really thought because I was a successful minister traveling and ministering to thousands of people around the world.

Now my approach is different. I write this book as a person who discovered his own need to overcome the effects of disappointment. Because of my success-coaching business I have studied some psychology, but my approach to gaining freedom is not as much based in psychology as it is biblical and theological.

The Bible speaks often on the subject of disappointment. One example is the story of Sarah, the wife of Abraham who experienced major emotional flux when she and her husband were hoping to have a child. In the end Sarah overcame every challenge and gave birth to a son. The New Testament explains that when she reached the conclusion that God was faithful, she received His power to conceive (Heb. 11:11).

Sarah's steps to freedom reveal how we can overcome our disappointment. We will also learn from the wisdom of King David, who successfully resisted and defeated disappointment. Hidden in their stories is a three-part process of empowerment and victory that includes refusing to faint during adversity, choosing to believe that God is good, and yielding to the joy found in God's goodness. We will explore all three!

My hope is that all of us will see God's power break the chains of disappointment. Expect a dramatic shift in your perspective as you run head-on into His goodness.

Now if you are ready for a life worth celebrating, dive right into chapter 1!

Part One

I Almost Fainted

CELEBRATE GOD'S GOODNESS

G od is *good*. When a person has experienced disappointment, that's not always an easy thing to believe. We think He is good *sometimes* or to *some* people, but that is never true. God is a perfect father, and He is good *all the time.* It is impossible for Him to be or do anything bad. Bad is the product of evil, and God cannot be evil because He is righteous and always right.

Knowing that God is good is the first step in discovering the art of joy. It is the foundation upon which everything rests.

What I am about to say might jolt you and challenge your beliefs to the core, but it's true: God thinks only good things about you. No, don't fight it! Jeremiah says that He has only thoughts of good and not evil toward you; they are thoughts of an expected end (Jer. 29:11). This tells me that *we* should expect a good ending instead of a negative one.

If you and I are believers, our belief should be signified by a positive and uplifted view of things. This is God's vantage point, and we should have it. Natural circumstances have nothing to do with this outlook. God's viewpoint raises us up!

Before I came to believe in Jesus, I was fully reliant on my own skill set and abilities. From my natural perspective I alone could make things happen. But as a believer I must realize that I am not alone; God wants to be directly involved in my circumstances.

People often call the supernatural intervention of God His *favor*. If that is true, His favor manifests as His goodness in our lives. Yet many people believe that it is hard to find God and His favor, but why? Because God is a positive God, I believe only sin-consciousness can tempt us to reject this view of Him.

Every one of us can experience God's goodness firsthand. Favor is the manifestation of it; it is God's goodness in action. To have this life in us, all we have to do is put our faith in God. The following scripture makes it simple:

> He who earnestly *seeks good finds favor,* but trouble will come to him who *seeks evil.*
> —PROVERBS 11:27

Here we see that good is associated with favor, and trouble is associated with evil. It is clear cut: God cannot be evil, therefore He cannot be bad. This leaves only one option: *God is good.* And if we seek good, we will find God and His favor.

If you want to experience God's goodness, look for good in your life! Expect something good to show up in every circumstance. Seek a good God as you pray and read your Bible. Certain religious traditions and teachings have cast a bad light on God. If you study the Scriptures with good spiritual eyes, you will find a God who works earnestly to show us His goodness.

King David found this good God:

> I would have lost heart, unless I had believed that I would see the goodness of the LORD in the land of the living.
> —PSALM 27:13

When David wrote this, enemies were all around him. By natural appearances all hope was lost and David was going to die. Yet as a little boy David had developed the art of seeing every circumstance optimistically. He knew that God was easily found. He hit the nail on the head by saying, "I am believing to see the goodness of the Lord." He practiced the art of optimism based upon His trust in a good God.

Something good is coming *your* way. Look for good and you will easily entreat God. Keep expecting it, no matter what your circumstances look like. And always rejoice in God's goodness. Scripture tells us this is what God's saints are called to do:

> Now therefore, *arise*, O LORD God, to Your resting place, You and the ark of Your strength. Let Your priests, O LORD God, be clothed with salvation, and let *Your saints rejoice in goodness.*
> —2 CHRONICLES 6:41

This verse conveys the idea that God will not rest until His saints rejoice in His goodness. The story is never finished until God's goodness is revealed. Things might look bleak, but that only means God is not yet enthroned on your praises, as the Bible says He should be (Ps. 22:3).

We must learn to praise the Lord for His goodness before we see the victory. God moves toward us when we agree with and applaud His ability to perform in our lives. Praising Him beforehand is a sign of our agreement that He can do the impossible. And when we praise Him—not because we want Him to "perform" but because He is worthy—He brings the victory and takes His resting place, His throne.

Let all His saints worldwide rejoice, sing, clap, shout, and laugh because God truly is good all the time…and, yes, all the time, God is good. His saints, His true believers, are like David; they have developed the art of believing in His goodness no matter the circumstances.

The Key of David

It can be easier to say, "No matter what," than to live it, especially when you're in the middle of disappointing circumstances. In 1 Samuel 30 David lost everyone and everything he loved. Even the mighty men who stood by him in battle threatened to stone him to death. Yet David knew the key to victory. He knew how to build a throne no matter what the issue was. The key of David's victories has always been to build a throne *through praise*.

Look at this verse with me:

> Now David was greatly distressed, for the people spoke of stoning him, because the soul of all the people was grieved, every man for his sons and his daughters. *But David strengthened himself in the Lord his God.*
>
> —1 Samuel 30:6

Notice that David wasn't distressed about his losses. I believe He knew he would get them back. Stress entered the picture when the men he'd always counted on turned against him.

Sometimes we trust in our strength and resources to deliver us from painful circumstances. We are sure of victory until the things we rely upon turn against us. That is when we must understand the truth about victory. It is the key David discovered—praising God releases victory.

The Scripture says that David encouraged himself by praising Elohim Yahweh, the Lord God. When you and I praise the ruler of the universe in the midst of every circumstance, we find our courage. When we enthrone God with our praise, we encourage ourselves.

We saints can anticipate a good outcome in every circumstance the Lord God is involved in. When our circumstances don't look like reasons to celebrate, we can celebrate the Lord's goodness because He is *always* good. When we focus on what is bad, trouble instantly reveals itself. But when we search for the good in our situations, favor always reveals itself.

Jesus said we would have tribulation in this world, but we are to be of good cheer because He has overcome it all (John 16:33). Bad things *will* show up, but we should not focus on them. Instead, we can encourage ourselves as we look to the God who is always good.

God desires to draw us by His goodness. Most people don't recognize God's goodness until they are desperate for salvation. Jeremiah 31:12 says that people will come streaming to the Lord's goodness, "their souls shall be like a well-watered garden, and they shall sorrow no more at all."

Can you imagine a life where we "sorrow no more at all"? In Jeremiah 31 God promised to comfort His people and turn their mourning into joy. Reading verses 12 through 14, I am strongly convinced that God does not want His people sad and sorrowful. Look at what He says in verse 14: "I will satiate the soul of the priests with abundance, and *My people shall be satisfied with My goodness,* says the LORD."

JOY, GOODNESS, AND JUSTICE

My dear friends Georgian and Winnie Banov are known as the Joy Apostles. God uses them to bring joy to the most tragic situations. Although they minister regularly in the United States, they spend much of their time reaching the broken, destitute, and forgotten people of the world.

Winnie is a hero! Given a choice about where to spend her time in ministry, she would choose a literal dump somewhere in a third-world country. Georgian and Winnie both spend much of their time reaching those who live, eat, work, and survive in the dumps—and they do it from within. Georgian and Winnie subject themselves to this way of living for the sole purpose of spreading Jesus's love and joy in places that would be hell to many.

It's amazing to see Winnie working with these people. People leave her presence wearing huge smiles. If you saw Winnie today you would not believe that she spent seven long years battling depression. Through the revelation of a good and joyful God, depression was destroyed in her life. The joy of her salvation and the revelation of the finished work of Christ have accomplished this.

You too can experience the finished work and live in absolute bliss with God no matter what your circumstances. It is found in completely believing that He is good—so good that He wants you to experience His goodness. Once you have this insight, goodness and its companion, mercy, will follow you (Ps. 23:6). Get their attention, and they will follow you all of the days of your life.

I had the privilege of preaching at a 107th birthday gathering for Otis "Dad" Clark, who was just seven years old when one of Christianity's most influential movements, the Azusa Street Revival, occurred. Dad Clark possessed a winning attitude. The words he spoke when he visited our church explain why: "If you are on the Lord's side, then you are on the winning side!" Dad Clark believed it. He knew beyond the shadow of a doubt that *God is good.*

If you know that, you will search for God's goodness in every circumstance. Whether you are looking for a parking spot or a job interview, you look for His favor, expecting Him to be good to you. You are on the winning side.

The following scripture describes this kind of living. Read it slowly and carefully. It should explode within you!

> And therefore the Lord [earnestly] waits [expecting, looking, and longing] to be gracious to you; and therefore He lifts Himself up, that He may have mercy on you and show loving-kindness to you. For the Lord is a God of justice. Blessed (happy, fortunate, to be envied) are all those who [earnestly] wait for Him, who expect and

look and long for Him [for His victory, His favor, His love, His peace, His joy, and His matchless, unbroken companionship]!

—ISAIAH 30:18, AMP

God is eager to be gracious to you. He is eager to be good to you. He is eager to show you His favor. He is eager to have mercy on you. If you question whether you deserve His goodness, just reread this part of the verse again: "He lifts Himself up, that He may have mercy on you and show loving-kindness to you. For the Lord is a God of justice."

God positions Himself above all circumstances so He can lift us to Himself. He is high above, so there is no one like Him. Only He is able to make the rules. The Bible says there is only one lawgiver and judge. There is only one justice. (See James 4:12.) No one has the last word but God Himself.

God lifts Himself to have mercy on us. He is bigger than our circumstances. But not only that, God also *thinks* bigger than we do. He is not moved by our circumstances or our failures.

When my children fail because of their lack of capacity to do better at a given point in time, I must be bigger for their sakes. I can only encourage them to do better if I am bigger than the circumstances they are experiencing. My elevation and vantage point allow me to make a judgment that their current aptitudes cannot conceive. This allows me to be merciful. A low, small-minded judge cannot have mercy because he or she lives at the level of the circumstance.

The bottom line is that God's goodness is unshakable, and we should attest to it. "Oh, give thanks to the LORD, for He is good! For His mercy endures forever" (Ps. 107:1). Those who do good things deserve our thanks. God *is* good. Not only are His actions good, but the word *good* also describes His character. Therefore we can count on Him to be consistently good and to display His goodness in unending mercy.

When I tell my kids that we are going to Disneyland, they immediately get excited, and they stay that way! They don't worry about whether I'll keep my promise. They never ask how much the plane tickets or Disneyland passes cost. They don't concern themselves with the hotel or restaurant bills. They could not care less about expenses. They just *believe* that they are going to Disneyland. They leave the details to their papa, trusting him to handle everything.

That's how we are to believe God. If He said it, we believe it—and that's that! He is good, His promises are good, and He will handle the details.

My wife's mother was a powerful woman of prayer—a powerhouse! Through her many challenges in life she developed a high level of trust in God's goodness. Being raised in World War II, she lacked many things. As a young girl tulip bulbs were her only food. Doctors said that if the war had not ended, she would have died of poisoning from the bulbs.

Later in life she was diagnosed with breast cancer. It had taken over her body and kept her in constant pain. My wife remembers sitting on her mother's lap as a child and not being able to lean back because of her mother's pain.

At some point the Lord asked my mother-in-law a simple question: "When are you healed? Is it when you feel healed or when I tell you that you are healed?"

Her reply was simple: "I am healed when You say I am healed!"

From that point forward she went on with her life and forgot about the cancer. Weeks passed without her checking for tumors or looking for pain. Then one day when she actually checked, all her pain was gone, *along with the tumors.*

Give thanks to the Lord, for He is good!

Chapter 2

FIND THE GOOD LIFE

In the Garden of Eden when God made us in His image and likeness, He intended for us to have His character, which is good. God never intended for us to be overwhelmed by bad people, situations, or experiences. Because sin entered the world, bad things will happen. But they don't have to define us. We can experience the good life God desires for us if we will get the right perspective.

We saw in the previous chapter that a good perspective can cause favor to manifest. But the opposite is also possible: the fallen nature and its unbelief attract the opposite of good. But if you will fight the urge to focus on negative things, you will see the miraculous results that come from your ultimate faith and trust in God.

We saw this verse earlier, but it bears repeating: "He who earnestly seeks *good* finds *favor,* but trouble will come to him who *seeks evil*" (Prov. 11:27). The simplicity of God's will is amazing. In Creation God used one word to express what He saw: *good.*

When He saw the light, it was good (Gen. 1:4). The darkness was evident, but God did not describe it. He intended for light to govern the darkness. Good is supposed to rule over bad. God's cheerleaders should ring louder than the devil's advocates. In God's kingdom light should never be washed out by darkness. Tribulation should never make us flinch.

"Then God *saw* everything that He had made, and indeed it was very good" (v. 31). God never called any part of His creation bad. Why? Because anything negative is subject to change. Negative circumstances are unfinished products. They cannot be good. In God's sight anything *not good* is a canvas waiting to become a work of art.

LIGHT AND DARKNESS

God gave us two options in life. One is to fix our eyes on God's best life for us. The other is to focus on experiencing both good and bad. These two choices are exemplified by two trees:

> Out of the ground the LORD God made to grow every tree that is pleasant to the sight and good for food. The *tree of life* was also in the midst of the garden, along with the *tree of knowledge of good and evil.*
> —GENESIS 2:9, MEV

The Hebrew word for evil simply denotes that which is bad. We can choose to be intimately acquainted with good and bad. This knowledge comes from the second tree in Genesis 2:9. Or we can recognize what is good as God's finished product, and what is bad as God's work in progress. The tree of life provides knowledge and intimate experience, but it is filled only with life.

We have to make this choice every day. Look around the room you are in. Unless you are sitting in total darkness, you will see the ruling power of light. When you turn off the light, darkness rules the room. As soon as you flip the light switch back on, darkness must surrender. Even children know this. That is why they ask for a night-light to be turned on.

God has never changed His mind about the supremacy of light over darkness. Never will we see darkness forcing light out of a room. The only way darkness can gain any authority at all is for us to shut out the light. This is also true in the one place where light and darkness have commingled since the Fall: within us. We must do what God did in the beginning: assert light's power over the darkness.

Let's go back to the garden for a moment. God told Adam and Eve not to eat of the second tree for a very specific reason:

> God knows that on the day you eat of it *your eyes will be opened* and you will be like God, *knowing* good and evil.
> —GENESIS 3:5, MEV

God knew that if Adam and Eve partook of the tree of the knowledge of good and evil, their eyes would be opened to things He never intended them to see. Seeing the goodness in life was God's best for them. But a third party exposed them to negativity, and they embraced the temptation. As a result evil is visible to us and we must contend with it.

Yes, our eyes have been opened to many negative and unwanted realities: failure, fear, doubt, unbelief, sickness, pain, shame, confusion, condemnation, hopelessness, and more. But life is good! As Matthew's Gospel explains, life's beauty is in the eye of the beholder:

> The lamp of the body is the eye. If therefore your eye is good, your whole body will be full of light. But if your eye is bad, your whole body will be full of darkness. If therefore the light that is in you is darkness, how great is that darkness!
> —MATTHEW 6:22–23

Both light and darkness have the same port of entry into our lives. What comes in depends upon the choices we make. The consequences can be profound.

> When *the woman saw that the tree was good for food*, that it was pleasing to the eyes and a tree desirable to make one wise, she took of its fruit and ate; and she gave to her husband with her, and he ate.
> —GENESIS 3:6, MEV

Eve made a choice based on her perception. She saw something good in what God said was not good for her. This is exactly how deception works; we call right wrong and wrong right. Our vision is impaired because we are deceived. This is why having a "God's-eye view" is so important. We live in His life-giving power when we agree with Him. What we agree with always determines how we live. "For as [a man] thinks in his heart, so is he" (Prov. 23:7, MEV).

You and I are what we think. If we think negatively in our hearts, we become negative. If we think good in our hearts, we are good. When I was young, I thought that I was stupid. When it was time to take a test, it seemed pointless to try, so I didn't. I bypassed the opportunity to succeed, telling myself, "I am stupid; therefore, I cannot answer the questions correctly."

In reality I was not intellectually stupid. I was stupid in my heart. As a result I became stupid in my life. Once I stopped believing the lie, I started getting different results. The Bible bears out this principle and has a great deal to say on the subject. The following verses shed much light:

> A good tree does not bear bad fruit, nor does a bad tree bear good fruit. For every tree is known by its own fruit. For men do not gather figs from thorns, nor do they gather grapes from a bramble bush. A good man out of the good treasure of his heart brings forth good;

and an evil man out of the evil treasure of his heart
brings forth evil. For out of the abundance of the heart
his mouth speaks.

—LUKE 6:43–45

An apple tree doesn't produce figs. Nor does a good person
purposely bring forth bad fruit. We bring forth whatever we
store up or *treasure* in our hearts. Good is different from bad in
this sense: good must be brought forth intentionally. Before we
can bring forth good, we must believe strongly that we are God's
answer for the evil in the world.

That takes intentionality.

CHOOSING WHAT YOU STORE UP

Life is what we make it. We can choose to use His life within
us to make good things happen around us. Bad things happen
every day, but we have the answer within. Therefore we have the
power to turn something bad into something good. According
to Luke 6:45, the heart-mouth connection is our starting point.
If our results in life are poor, we need to check our words. The
more we challenge what's coming out of our mouths, the more
we will change what is in our hearts. Changing our confession is
important, but so is depleting our storage of negativity. This happens when we stop speaking negatively.

When our words are positive, we store different values in our
hearts. Our words, in turn, reflect our hearts' new values. The
cycle is from the heart, to the mouth, into the ears, and then
back into the heart. We can affect change in the heart if we purposefully change our speech to match the Word of God.

As a success coach I listen for patterns of speech when con-
versing with those whom I coach. I can usually identify the
source of negative outcomes within a few short minutes.
Necessity might be the mother of invention, but repetition is the
mother of skill. I've learned that people tend to reiterate their

personal limits when they speak. They don't notice it, but they repeat their limits over and over again.

My job is to notice any productive or nonproductive patterns and build systems that either maximize or manage what is there. This can be done by devaluing what is negative, increasing the value in positive conversation, and building repetitious statements that produce beneficial results. I find that when my clients' speech is changed, the heart changes become visible in their posture and lightened emotional state.

Remember that you hear your own words, and you believe what you say more than you believe anyone else. There is an upside to this: you can store up good things in your heart by speaking good things into your own ears!

You can apply this truth starting with what you say about yourself. Speak good things about yourself, and those good things will become evident in your life. If your opinion of yourself is negative, trust in God! He will help you see the good He placed within you. You were created in His image and likeness, and they are both *very* good.

Here is some sound advice: quit being your own worst enemy. When you know that God has instilled good in you, you won't be concerned about what is happening around you.

Abraham's example is a good one. When God called Abraham to move away from his family, his nephew Lot went with him. Both men prospered greatly until the land they shared was not big enough to sustain both of them. Abraham gave Lot first dibs on the surrounding lands, and Lot selected the choicest piece (Gen. 13:9–11).

This was not an issue for Abraham. He did not feel cheated or disappointed because he knew he possessed the blessing. Wherever Abraham went, the blessing from the Lord would be with him. If he ended up in the desert, it would become an oasis because of what he believed about himself and about God.

Abraham trusted the Lord to make streams in the desert; but Lot placed his trust in a good tract of land.

In the end Lot found only trouble, and Abraham lived an even more blessed life. What each man had stored up in his heart showed up in his circumstances.

A LIFE AS GOOD AS YOU MAKE IT

Life is what you make it. If you have the best breaks and the most unique gifts and talents, you will squander them unless you see the good God has placed within you. It happens every day; talented people miss amazing opportunities simply because they don't see clearly. Their perspectives dictate their outcomes.

This does not have to happen to you. You are more like Abraham than Lot. You have God's promised blessing and goodness on your life. As Paul explained in his letter to Titus: "To the pure all things are pure, but to those who are defiled and unbelieving nothing is pure; but even their mind and conscience are defiled" (Titus 1:15). Pure-hearted people see the pure within every circumstance. They are guided by a clean heart and undefiled conscience.

I read a story about perspective in Rabbi Moshe Gans's book *Success!* Gans wrote about two Bible students who approached their teacher with a question: "The Talmud tells us that we must bless Hashem for misfortune with the same happiness that we bless Him for good fortune. How is it possible to do this?"[1]

Their teacher told them to visit Reb Zushe, an extremely poor man who often lacked life's basic necessities yet was always happy. The two brothers told Reb Zushe why their teacher thought he should answer their question. Reb Zushe was puzzled and said, "I am surprised that the Maggid sent you to me. You should really speak with someone who has experienced suffering in his life. As for me, I have only experienced good things. Nothing bad has ever happened to me."[2]

Perspective is everything. Someone with a pure perspective will find what is pure in every circumstance. A person who is defiled and unbelieving cannot recognize God in anything—not even in the most favorable circumstances. According to Titus 1:15, unbelief and impurity are the same thing; believing and purity are the same thing; and a pure conscience is a believing heart and mind.

Paul the apostle encouraged us to live with a pure, believing mind-set, and he explained how:

> Finally, brethren, whatever things are *true*, whatever things are *noble*, whatever things are *just*, whatever things are *pure*, whatever things are *lovely*, whatever things are *of good report*, if there is *any virtue* and if there is anything *praiseworthy—meditate* on these things.
>
> —PHILIPPIANS 4:8

We must meditate on information and facts in order to extract virtue from them. When we fail to consider how God will use life's situations, our emotions will legitimize and log them. The Greek word translated "meditation" or "think" is *logizomai*.[3] Its definition is evident in the word's first three letters. It means to "reckon, count…calculate."

We must catalog things intentionally and purposefully. Unless we attach a purpose to our circumstances, a negative connotation will be assigned, whether by default or the devil. We need to be proactive in this, as the late healing evangelist Oral Roberts was. Whenever undesirable circumstances happened in Brother Roberts's life, he quickly cataloged them saying, "God knows something about this we don't know."[4] That immediately closed the door on any voice beside God's.

In *Success!* Rabbi Gans tells another story, this time about a poverty-stricken man named Nachum:

He was blind, his legs were amputated, and he lived
in a house fit to be condemned. Nonetheless, Nachum
responded to every distressful event with the words,
Gam zu letovah (this is also for the good). He saw events
better, he found a benefit in every event, even if the
event seemed negative.[5]

Life is good, but how we see it depends upon what we think.
When we look for good, we find it in every circumstance. The
same is true of how we see ourselves. We are whatever we meditate on. As we think…as we catalog…in our minds and hearts,
so are we!

Chapter 3

LOOK ON THE RIGHT SIDE

The right side is the bright side of things. It is more than positive thinking; it is possibility thinking. It means standing on the Lord's side—the winning side—and seeing things as He does. This is the *only* way to see the bright side.

To do this and to really win in life, we must first belong to God. His desire and His plan are for us to experience all the good things He has already prepared. Yes, there will be challenges to our faith in Him and His goodness, but we must keep looking for the right outcome that God has in mind.

Remember that what we seek determines what we find. "He who earnestly seeks good finds favor, but trouble will come to him who seeks evil" (Prov. 11:27). The phrase "earnestly seeks good" is just one word in the Hebrew. It means to "search for" or "enquire early,"[1] "look early, diligently for"[2] (in this case to seek *good* diligently, early, and earnestly).

We should wake up in the morning saying, "Something good is going to happen to me today!" When starting new jobs, we should look for promotion from the beginning. When we start new businesses, we should expect them to prosper at the outset.

For many years I wondered how people found favor on their lives. The secret is in Proverbs 11:27; it essentially tells us to look earnestly and early for good things to happen and we will find favor. Notice that I did not say, "Look for favor and favor will come." The idea is to look for *good* and favor will come!

Keep looking for good in your marriage and you will find favor in your marriage. It is easy to complain about things that are not right. You don't have to look for them; they will announce themselves. Looking for the good in your marriage is less automatic; it must be done habitually and on purpose.

When we cultivate this viewpoint, we exact favor; but when we are focused on the negatives, we tend to miss opportunities for favor. It is when we change what we are looking for that favor, by definition, shows up with pleasure, delight, goodwill, and acceptance, and changes our will and our desire too.

A young single mom in our church experienced this favor firsthand. After she gave her life to Christ, she began expecting good things to happen. She worked in the makeup section of a prominent department store. When she adopted a mind-set of looking for good, good things happened, and she became the number one salesperson in her department.

This continued for many months. The transformation was so dramatic and her sales increased at such a pace that her boss asked whether she had been taking sales training or Toastmasters' classes. The single mother's response was simple and direct: "I have favor."

Her supervisor's response was classic: "Who is doing you a favor?"

That literally makes me laugh out loud! The young lady knew she had found favor. Her sales record was proof. She never expected favor; she expected good things. God loves when we look for good things to happen—and He responds.

Remember that God longs to be gracious; He looks for opportunities to be good to those who expect and look and long for His graciousness and goodness. Are you one of them?

HIS MIND IN US

Seeing the right side of things is especially critical in crisis times. One day Pharaoh became so angry with his butler and baker that he sent both of them to prison. The captain of the prison guard assigned Joseph to serve the two men. One morning Joseph found them downcast and asked, "Why do you look so sad today?" (Gen. 40:7).

Joseph was accustomed to seeing the good in every circumstance. But obviously something was wrong this day. Soon he learned that both men had had disturbing dreams—so disturbing that it affected their countenance.

The men were in a bad way and realized they had nothing to lose, so they told Joseph what troubled them. Joseph in turn sought God's counsel and ministered truth to the men. There is a lesson here for us: when distressing events occur, we must realize we have nothing to lose and much to gain. We must look for good in the midst of our turmoil, and we will find favor. Just as Joseph sought God's heart for the answers, we too must go to God for answers.

Philippians 2:5 says: "Let this mind be in you which was also in Christ Jesus." The Greek word *phroneo* is translated "let mind be." It sticks out to me because it speaks of permission. In other words we have to *permit* the mind of Christ to take over our thinking.

Phroneo goes beyond permission, however. It also means:

> To have understanding, be wise...to feel, to think...to have an opinion of oneself, think of oneself...to be modest, not to let one's opinion (though just) of himself

> exceed the bounds of modesty...to be of the same mind,
> i.e., to agree together, cherish the same views...[3]

Even if our opinions of ourselves are true, we must not allow them to reflect on the real power and glory that we possess in Christ. We must resist and empty ourselves, as Christ emptied Himself of reputation.

Do you remember how many times Jesus told people not to reveal who healed them? Jesus did not seek recognition. When He found a man who could not get himself into the healing waters of the pool, Jesus told him to stand up and go home. (See John 5.) The man obeyed and was made whole. Jesus never introduced Himself to the man. He wasn't seeking recognition; He was simply doing good (Acts 10:38).

In another instance Jesus encountered demonic spirits and prevented them from speaking because they knew who He was (Mark 1:34). Jesus didn't want everyone to know His status. He wanted to do good without making a big deal of Himself.

Let the same attitude be in us that was in Jesus. If we lose our desire for notoriety and self-importance, we will also lose our tendency toward self-preservation. Kingdom life is for those who do not love their lives even unto death (Rev. 12:11).

I would dare say that all of life's stresses are related to our attempts to increase our status and/or save our lives. Stress is often a by-product of want and lack. God has promised to provide for all our needs. He is our shepherd and supplier. When I find myself in want of something, I check my heart. Somewhere I have developed a desire that didn't come from the Lord. Somehow I have lost the heart of a servant and gained a heart of lust. But when I possess the mind of a son and the heart of a servant, I discover the power to overcome everything.

My middle child, Yosef, lives this way. He has a calling of increase and is naturally generous. His giving has to be watched or he will give everything away and be left with nothing. When he and his siblings were young, we would stop for fast food as we traveled from city to city. Each child would order a meal with a toy and open his or her bag immediately to find it.

Yosef's order was consistently messed up. He would look in the bag and exclaim, "I have two toys!" It happened all the time. Without fail he gave one of the toys to a sibling.

Gifts are Yosef's love language. He serves everyone around him through giving. He is also the happiest and most carefree boy I have ever met. He hasn't a worry; therefore he has no need or desire to build a reputation for himself. He doesn't care if you like him or not. He is too happy being generous and free. If he falls and you laugh, he will fall again just to bring you joy. He doesn't get embarrassed because he doesn't think of himself. This makes him free from the social norms that hinder generosity and worry minds.

Scripture describes Yosef's way of thinking: "For 'who has known the mind of the LORD that he may instruct Him?' But we have the mind of Christ" (1 Cor. 2:16). Yosef's generosity reflects God's thinking. Some religious traditions teach that He wants to subtract from us. Some movies show worshippers sacrificing people to volcanos to prevent eruptions. They depict God as a taker. But a study of God's mind and character reveal a God who adds. When He intervened at the Tower of Babel, He did not subtract languages; He added them (Gen. 11).

Those who know God understand His mind and make their choices accordingly. Because He is positive, we can live free of negative thinking and instead possess possibility thinking. Jesus was so possibility-minded that not even death could hold Him down. In Acts 2:24 Luke described Jesus "whom God raised up by loosening the pull of death, because it was not possible that He should be held by it" (MEV). Jesus confidently said in John 10:18 that He laid His life down willingly, and no one could take it from Him.

You have the same mind as Jesus and the same superior DNA! That DNA ensured that Jesus would never be overcome by *anything.* Likewise, it is impossible for anything to overcome you, unless you give your permission.

NOT DOUBLE-MINDED

Possibility thinkers are intolerant toward negativity. In fact, they detest it. We are encouraged in Romans 12:9 to "abhor evil and cling to what is good." The word *abhor* means to hate extremely, or have contempt; it means to "cast away, reject, despise, defy, contemn, loathe...detest,"[4] "despise [and] abominate."[5]

Have you ever noticed how sensitive babies' taste buds are? To them, sweet is very sweet and bitter is very bitter. When my son Tristen was a baby, he would devour sweet potatoes but spit out his green beans. He would pucker his lips so tightly that we rarely fed him another spoonful. If we managed to sneak one in, he would spit it out and wipe his tongue. He abhorred the bitter and clung to the sweet. Scripture encourages us to do the same: abhor what is evil and cling to what is good.

We cannot love good *and* bad. That is double-mindedness, which we are admonished not to have. Notice what the psalmist said about double-mindedness: "I hate those who are double-minded, but I love Your law" (Ps. 119:113, MEV). The psalmist loved the law because it was directly opposed to evil. The apostle James also felt strongly about double-mindedness. He said, "A double-minded man is unstable in all his ways" (James 1:8, MEV). In James 4:8 he wrote: "Draw near to God, and He will draw near to you. Cleanse your hands, you sinners, and purify your hearts, you double-minded" (MEV). James was clear: we can't love both good and bad. We must either become conscious of one or the other.

Matthew chapter 21 describes two sons who were invited to help their father in the vineyard. The first son said he would not assist; the second said he would. Neither son kept his word. The son who declined the invitation showed up to help. The one who promised to help never did. Both sons were double-minded, but the first one became obedient. This tells me that we can repent of double-mindedness and align ourselves with doing the Father's will instead.

Notice that the psalmist's hatred of the double-minded (Ps. 119:113) was not demonic, but godly. God hates evil, and so should we. We need to reject bad thoughts, emotions, and patterns—we should *hate* them. This hatred is a powerful emotion that must be intentionally directed. It cannot be granted its own reign; it is to rise up when evil is present. That being said, we are not to hate people but the activity and results of evil.

At the same time we are to embrace everything that is good. We are called to focus on good, do good, look for good (by looking past whatever is bad). This is how we overcome evil, including disappointment: we look for good things to celebrate, and we look for more good things to come.

When we do this, God performs miracles. Bible teacher Joyce Meyer shares an amazing example of this from the life of Smith Wigglesworth:

> Smith Wigglesworth was a great preacher. But before he was a preacher, he was a plumber who wasn't a Christian—or a very nice man. Fortunately for him, he had a godly wife. He didn't want her to go to church, but she went anyway. When she did, he'd lock her out of the house, and when she came home, she'd have to sleep on the back porch. In the morning he'd unlock the door and she'd come in and say, "Good morning, Smithy!" and make him breakfast.[6]

Good is God's power to override the bad. Jesus provides us with His overcoming power in John 16:33: "I have told you these things so that in Me you may have peace. In the world you will have tribulation. But be of good cheer. I have overcome the world" (MEV). This verse teaches us three things. First, we see that when we trust Jesus's words, we will possess His peace.

Second, we must be of good cheer. Third, Jesus has dominance over the world.

We tap into Christ's peace and authority to overcome by being of good cheer. It may seem naïve to believe that being cheerful can accomplish this. It would be naïve, *if* we were simply trying to be happy in the midst of tragedy. The reality is that we are cheering up because Jesus has already overcome death, hell, the grave, cancer, poverty, relationship problems, financial issues, ignorance, hatred, pain, shame, lack of direction, etc. Jesus has already triumphed over *any* trouble that is found in the world. We respond to problems with good cheer *because* of this.

If we trust His words, Jesus will come and deliver us.

LIVING ON THE RIGHT SIDE

When Jesus approached the tomb of Lazarus He had one thing in mind: to raise Lazarus from the grave (John 11). Jesus didn't think something good *might* happen. He approached the tomb with absolute faith, fully expecting a beneficial outcome. Jesus wasn't simply being positive or looking on the bright side; He was looking on the *right* side of things, seeing them as God saw them. The definition of *good* conveys the idea of righteousness. God is righteous because His way is *always* right. When we search out the good in every circumstance, we look for righteousness to prevail. This activates the power of righteousness that brings all things into a right state.

Jesus showed that miracles follow when we search for good. That does not mean He overlooked the difficulties, challenges, and hurts. As our substitute Jesus had to feel our infirmities before overcoming them (Heb. 4:15). I believe Jesus delayed going to Lazarus because He needed to feel the loss of someone He loved. Jesus wept for Lazarus as the Son of Man, but He overcame weeping as the Son of God (see John 11:35–44). When He said, "Father, You always hear Me; I say this for the sake of those around Me" (see verses 41–42), He revealed that He did what He did for the sake of those who were present and those who would read about it later.

Because Jesus wept as the Son of Man and overcame sorrow and grief as the Son of God, His death on the cross gives us the power and courage to do the same. We are no longer obligated to handle life's tribulations as mere men but as children of God. Jesus did more than put an end to the grieving over Lazarus; He made sure that everyone involved understood that they needed only to *believe*. Believing under difficult circumstances is not the norm in our society. Instead it is courageous. This courage in the midst of trials, pain, hopelessness (when courage is *not* the norm), can only happen when our faith is anchored in the supernatural intervention of God. A paraphrase of Jesus's words in John 16:33 tells us what this courage looks like: "In this world you will have tribulation, but be cheerful; I have overcome it all." This is the courage He gives us: the ability to be cheerful during trials. In the midst of tribulation our righteous courage overcomes all!

This courage comes in many forms. Have you ever seen someone laugh in the face of danger? Or stand up to a bully? Or risk his or her own life to save someone else's? Have you ever seen people smile when they should be grieving? These are outward expressions of an inward, righteous courage.

"Cheer up" is Jesus's prescription for those who face difficult challenges. He told a paralyzed man, "Son, *be of good cheer;* your sins are forgiven you" (Matt. 9:2). The man received forgiveness when he chose righteous courage. When a woman with an issue of blood came to Jesus after spending all her money on doctors, He said, "Daughter, be of good cheer. Your faith has made you well. Go in peace" (Luke 8:48, mev). The moment she embraced righteous courage, she received peace in her body, finances, and life!

Do you remember what Jesus told His disciples when they saw Him walking on water and thought He was a ghost? He said, "*Be of good cheer!* It is I. Do not be afraid" (Matt. 14:27, mev).

The disciples learned how not to fear as they received righteous courage. They displayed the same faith when speaking to a blind man: "They called the blind man, saying to him, *'Be of good cheer. Rise, He is calling you'"* (Mark 10:49). The blind man received his sight as He approached Jesus with righteous courage.

Once, when Paul the apostle was in jail, Jesus paid him a special visit. He stood near Paul and comforted him, saying, *"Be of good cheer,* Paul; for as you have testified for Me in Jerusalem, so you must also bear witness at Rome" (Acts 23:11). Through righteous courage, Paul received strength to finish his life's journey.

Paul carried the torch to those whom he met along the way. Once, when a hurricane at sea made shipwreck seem inevitable, Paul told the frightened crew: "Wherefore, sirs, *be of good cheer:* for I believe God, that it shall be even as it was told me" (Acts 27:25, NAS). God told Paul they would not perish; the apostle was immovable and unshakable in believing Him and encouraged the others to remain righteously courageous.

The Bible reveals patterns of how our lives should be. When we believe in God's goodness, we are of good courage, no matter what circumstances face us. Whether we are afraid and superstitious as the disciples or the blind man were, whether we are like Paul, unfairly thrown in prison or caught in life-threatening storms, we can look on the right side of things and see the brighter side of life that He prepared for us.

Be of good cheer and have courage! Your circumstances may seem unfair, but be cheerful anyway. You will never have what is fair and good until you develop a clear picture of what is right in God's eyes. Then in righteous courage you will expect and receive miracles!

Chapter 4

AGREE WITH THE VOICE OF FAITH

Before we can be disappointed, we have to agree with the voice of disappointment, which is the voice of reason. We are called instead to agree with God. To do that, we must agree with the voice of faith.

In the end we partner with whatever or whoever gets our agreement. Many voices speak into our lives each day. For better or worse each has its own effect. If we learn to agree with God, His Word, and His purpose for our lives, we will disagree with reason and circumstance. Then our faith cannot be shipwrecked and disappointment cannot survive.

All relationships are based on agreement. The greater the agreement, the stronger a relationship becomes. The moment the parties cease to agree, the relationship begins breaking down. It is best to agree quickly with those who are right—and God is always right. Jesus is *Emmanuel*, "God with us" (Matt. 1:23). To walk with Him, we must agree with Him.

"Can two walk together, except they be agreed?" (Amos 3:3, KJV). The answer is *no*.

The word *agree* speaks of advancing, being of one mind, and harmonizing in opinion.[1] We don't agree just to be agreeable. All of our agreement should lead to advancement. We agree with God, His ways, and His words even when others find that "disagreeable."

Agreeing with God doesn't sit well with independent personalities. We cannot be independent and agree with God. This agreement is fully dependent upon our willingness to submit to Him, as the lesser to the greater. When we submit to God, we have His power to advance; it confirms that we were designed to be mastered by Him.

Unbelievers are led by something unreliable: their circumstances, or whatever seems sensible. We cannot afford to trust in unreliable things. Instead we trust in God and His Word, and through them we enjoy life and peace. But God's Word is more than information; it is also power. When we trust Him, we learn that His power *will* fulfill His promises.

This is exactly what the devil wants us *not* to do. He prefers us to be led by circumstances because he uses them to instill fear. The enemy wants to train our minds in darkness. He wants us to agree with him because he knows such agreement will advance fear, doubt, and unbelief.

God's agenda is not against us as Satan's is. God is for us! Still, we must choose to agree with Him and to renew our minds so we remain in agreement. Romans 12:2 reveals two forms of mind renewal. It says: "Do not be conformed to this world, but be transformed by the renewing of your mind, that you may prove what is the good and acceptable and perfect will of God" (MEV).

We can either agree by being conformed to the world's ways, or we can agree with God and be transformed. The Greek word translated "be conformed" means "to conform oneself (i.e. one's mind and character) to another's pattern (fashion one's self according to)…"[2] The Greek word used for "transform" means "to change into another form, to transform, to transfigure."[3]

When we live according to our circumstances, we conform to their standards. We renew our minds to the world's way of dealing with the issues. This is how unbelievers live. But God doesn't use circumstances to conform us; His way is to transform us into His image and likeness through His Word. In every situation God wants to renew and renovate our minds to be like His.

CONFORMED OR TRANSFORMED?

It is easy to recognize the starting point of disagreement, even without the benefit of voice inflections and body language. The telltale sign is the question, "Why?"

Why is the first opposing thought. In a single syllable it verbalizes our independence. When my kids realized that they could think on their own, they tested the waters by asking, "Why?" When Nathalie and I answered one question, they would ask another. If we had allowed it, the questioning would have been endless.

We are more likely to conform to ideas we understand, even if we do not understand at first. Ideas that originate with God are higher than our human thoughts. That means we don't always understand them fully. However, if we establish the fact that He is always right, we will put our faith in His way of thinking, despite any lack of understanding. This causes us to be transformed.

God is not trying to conform our minds so that we pretend or mirror Him. He wants to fully transform our thinking so that our ways and thoughts are higher than those of people who don't know Him. Remember: God wants to advance us. When we respond and think as the world does, we cheat ourselves. We take a step down from our place of privilege, which is to have the mind of Christ.

The mind of Christ allows us to discern right and wrong, and good and bad. The apostle Paul said in no uncertain terms that believers "have the mind of Christ" (1 Cor. 2:16). If you are a believer, that means *you*! So how are you using Christ's mind?

Jesus never trusted His circumstances above what His Father told Him. When the enemy paraded his ideas before Jesus, Jesus refused to be conformed to them. He rejected Satan and proclaimed God's Word (Matt. 4:4, 7, 10).

As Joshua prepared for the battle of Jericho, a man with a drawn sword appeared. With confidence and authority, Joshua asked, "Are you on our side or the enemy's side?" (See Joshua 5:13.)

With conviction, the man answered, "I am the Commander of the Lord's army." (See Josh. 5:14.) Until this moment Joshua almost certainly thought *he* was the commander of the Lord's army! But the real commander was leading Joshua into transformation. Next, he told Joshua to take off his shoes because he was standing on holy ground (v. 15).

When did Jericho become holy ground? Could it be that the ground became holy when Joshua realized that his destiny involved something bigger than what he thought? Isn't that what happened when Moses removed his shoes as he was commissioned to bring Israel out of bondage?

Both men had to remove their shoes in order for God's purposes to be achieved in ways only He could understand. You and I have to remove what we have known in order to achieve what has never been done. Jericho was a fortified city that had never been penetrated by an army. Joshua approached the place expecting "war as usual." But this wasn't going to be the usual war. This was work only the Lord could do. It was holy, meaning, "separated"; it was set apart to Joshua at the foundations of the world. No one else could lead this battle. Even Joshua could not do it without coming completely under the Lord's instruction.

God's man could not be conformed to the world's wisdom; he had to be transformed by God's thinking.

The Lord laid out His entire strategy (Josh. 6:1–5). No commander in the world, not even Joshua, would have imagined such a plan. Imagine marching around a city and expecting to win it! But Joshua followed God's instructions perfectly and won. The Lord's ways are always higher than our ways. To win holy battles, we need to strip off our human knowledge and let God's mind be in us.

SEPARATED AND SWEPT CLEAN

AS FAITHFUL AS Joshua and Moses were, they lacked the benefit of the new covenant in Jesus's blood. Scripture says it is a better covenant with better promises (Heb. 7:22; 8:6). Because of Jesus we can let His mind be in us in advance of our trials. Then when tribulation comes, we immediately have the power to overcome.

Jesus invited us to live in this grace:

> Are you tired? Worn out? Burned out on religion? Come to me. Get away with me and you'll recover your life. I'll show you how to take a real rest. Walk with me and work with me—watch how I do it. Learn the unforced rhythms of grace. I won't lay anything heavy or ill-fitting on you. Keep company with me and you'll learn to live freely and lightly.
> —MATTHEW 11:28–30, THE MESSAGE

The burden-free life is available when we yield to the mind of Christ and take off our "old shoes."

From the foundations of the world we were chosen to live in the specific grace by which we can achieve the holy and separated purpose ordained for each of us. King David understood this. He knew he had been separated by God for something unique. He was confident that He walked in God's purpose, therefore he would not accept any other plan or report. When enemies surrounded him, he took command of his emotions, saying, "I had fainted, unless I had believed to see the goodness of the LORD in the land of the living" (Ps. 27:13, KJV).

Had David lacked this level of confidence in what God had prepared and preserved for him, his often dire circumstances would have caused him to faint. But David already believed that God had something good planned for his future. Therefore there was no room in his mind for defeat. His heart was full of expectation, so there was no room for fainting.

When your "house" is already filled as David's was, there is no vacancy for anything other than God's victorious plan to occupy. Keep your house filled with hope, faith, and love; then defeat, fainting, and disappointment will be shut out. God has planned something good for you. It is on the other side of this trial. This momentary confusion and disappointment cannot disrupt God's plan, unless you allow it.

We know what we are full of by what spills out of our mouths. If we are full of doubt, doubt comes out. When we are full of faith, faith flows from our lips. If we are negative or disappointed, our words reveal it.

We can control our mouths when others are around, at least to a point. So here's my question: What's coming out of your mouth when no one is around? What does your self-talk sound like? Pay attention because your self-talk is key to how you live and what you receive in life.

Psalm 27:13 wasn't an act; it was King David's self-talk, and it affected his outcomes. Most of us are more careful when speaking to others. We really need to be more careful of what we say when we are alone. Those are the words that direct our lives. If we stay pregnant with hope, our self-talk will overflow with it and disappointment cannot enter our thinking.

Have you read the Bible story about the house that was swept clean? (See Matthew 12; Luke 11.) If your "house" is filled with disappointment, you must clean it out. We can sweep out our disappointment simply because we are tired of it. Isn't that what we do in the springtime? We are tired of whatever has been accumulating, so we clean it out.

We don't have to have all the answers before we start cleaning. Recently my sons and I cleaned our garage. There were certain things we knew had to be thrown out immediately. We were not as sure about other items. As we continued the process, the decisions became easier to make. When we were done, the garage was in order.

When you start cleaning out your disappointment and frustration, your Comforter will show you what to throw out and what to keep. The process starts when you decide that you are finished with the junk. Then the Holy Spirit comes to help you, just as my sons helped me with the garage. Because He knows you are committed to the task, He will assist in completing it.

The Bible story about the swept house doesn't explain why it got cleaned out. It only tells us that the junk was gone. But the house was left completely empty. Whoever cleaned the place did not expect guests to come or for the house to be put to good purpose. As a result, spiritual squatters came and the condition of the place was worse than before it was swept.

Don't just clean your spiritual house; envision what you will invite in when the cleaning is done. Fill it with expectation. Start dreaming again. Don't get free for the sake of being free; get free so you can *do something* with your freedom. Get in agreement with the voice of faith, and God's plan will play out.

When you sweep out the debris of disappointment, something else will leave with it: a victim mind-set. You have victory in Jesus! The mind of Christ is not a victim's mind, but a *victor's* mind.

Before Abraham's wife, Sarah, fully embraced God's promise of a son, she nursed a victim mind-set and acted upon it:

> Now Sarai, Abram's wife, had borne him no children. She had a female Egyptian servant whose name was Hagar. And Sarai said to Abram, "Behold now, the LORD has prevented me from bearing children. Go in to my

servant; it may be that I shall obtain children by her."
And Abram listened to the voice of Sarai.

                                        —GENESIS 16:1–2, ESV

The victim-minded person believes that God is preventing him from having or experiencing good things in life. Sarah allowed her circumstances to dictate her perception of God. Her troubles convinced her that He was the problem.

Most often we come into agreement with a thought or opinion through verbal and nonverbal communication. We read other people's speech and body language, and they read ours to interpret our state of mind and our intent. Sarah had God's promise in words but lacked instruction on how to bring it to pass. She assumed that her continued barrenness was God's nonverbal expression that He had rejected her. Nonverbal communication is tricky enough; assuming that circumstances express God's intended meaning is even worse. Sarah misread the "signs." God had not withdrawn His promise or rejected her.

SATAN'S VOICE

There are only two voices in the world: God's and Satan's. All other voices speak in agreement with one or the other.

Since the Garden of Eden Satan has used other people's voices to convey his desires and plans. His greatest weapon is disguise. He is of darkness and must continue to operate within its borders. In order to be effective, Satan must use someone else's voice. In the garden he used the snake. Today he uses loved ones, friends, those whom we respect, and even a person's internal voice to convey his mind-set.

Read Sarah's story from Genesis 16:2–3 again. Notice the two voices. The first was the voice of disappointment declaring, "Behold now, *the Lord* has prevented me from bearing children" (ESV). Next came the voice of reason, saying, "Go in to my servant; it may be that I shall obtain children by her" (ESV).

Reasoning is a form of rationalization—the use of people, places, and circumstances to justify one's actions. Sarah had seen God's miracles firsthand. When her husband deceived Pharaoh by saying he and Sarah were siblings, God miraculously delivered her from Pharaoh's bed! (See Genesis 12.)

Despite all that Sarah knew about God, another voice of reason influenced her: it was the voice of presumption. Sarah developed her "Hagar strategy" to achieve God's promise, but she did it without God's permission. Every promise from God has a plan designed by Him to bring it to pass. Satan will always oppose that plan.

Sarah and Abraham lacked certain benefits we enjoy today. They did not have God's written Word to guide them. Nor did they have the Holy Spirit's leading from within or the fruit of the Spirit as we do now. Therefore Satan's voice was harder to discern. So Sarah accepted the idea that God rejected her.

Satan's clever use of circumstances convinced her of it. He used her external circumstances to support an internal voice of disappointment. This is an easy ploy when frustration is ripe. It was no doubt frustrating for Sarah to have a promise without knowing when, where, or how it would to come to pass. She and her husband had lived unparalleled lives of faith—yet even she surrendered to disappointment!

Up to this point in Abraham and Sarah's story, Abraham's display of faith was solid. It was not enough to sustain Sarah, however. At some point the individual must take ownership of the promise by his or her own faith, especially when other personal issues factor in. Sarah's lifelong battle with infertility served to dilute her faith in the promise. Her first recorded words regarding the promise were based in rejection, which serves only to tamp down faith.

The opening verse of Genesis 16 reveals what went wrong: "Now Sarai, Abram's wife, had borne him no children. She had a female Egyptian servant whose name was Hagar" (ESV). Sarah had always been barren, yet she had a promise of motherhood. It was not Abraham's job, Sarah's responsibility, or Hagar's privilege to "work" the promise. The miracle of a child was God's to perform.

When Satan's voice gets our attention, we can mistakenly assume responsibility for the promise instead of simply trusting God to be faithful. Immediately internal voices take control and build reasonings and rationalizations to describe how the promise will or will not come to pass. Too often it seems more satisfying to get busy "working the promise" than to trust the One who gave it.

The biggest danger with the internal voice is its tendency to sound like you. When the enemy speaks in voices of false hope, presumption (the perversion of faith), distress, assumption, condemnation, pride, and rejection, to name a few, he uses words and sounds that trick you into thinking the thoughts are yours. His mission is to lead you away from the comfort of God's love into a place a fear and confusion. Lying voices can never lead you toward the fulfillment of God's promise.

If you are still scratching your head and thinking that Satan's voice is not found in Sarah's story, you are partially right. His voice was used only indirectly. Remember that Satan is a master of disguise. War—of the mind or spirit, of words or of the world—boils down to the fact that there is God and a devil. We continually choose between them, either obeying one voice or the other.

In this battle we must remember that we are not self-sufficient. Not only do we choose the voices we follow, but we are also always reliant, either on God or on Satan. When we rely on God, we function at whatever level of sovereignty He allows. When we rely on the devil, we are governed by his whims and plans. Our choice is influenced by the voices we hear and believe. We might trust in God's goodness but if we allow it, the voice of our circumstances will corrode our trust and corrupt our faith.

Ten years of waiting in the land of Canaan "spoke" to Sarah. She watched as her husband (a good man who remained faithful to the promise) waited but did not receive the promise. Sarah obviously loved her husband. Her love and desire to please him may have prompted her to dwell on her disappointment. It probably seemed as if everything else in their lives was lining up, except for this one very important issue.

Can you relate to Sarah's plight? Often it is not what we have that brings disappointment; it's what we don't yet have. If we are not careful, we become discontented when God's promises take too long for our liking. When contentment leaves, it means we have abandoned our trust in God's goodness.

This is what happened to Sarah. She believed that God would use Hagar to bring forth a child, but not her. Sarah placed her faith in Hagar's ability simply because it was another option. Sadly it resulted in a pregnancy that had nothing to do with God's promise. There is a big difference between what is permissible (an alternate option) and what is promised (God's plan). The difference brought much grief to everyone involved.

Both Hagar and Sarah would experience childbirth, but Sarah's had a time stamp ordained by God. God's appointed time is part of the price of His promise. Every one of His promises has an appointed time and requires His intervention. Hagar had no promise from God about her children. Therefore her pregnancy could be performed by an act of the flesh. Sarah's child was promised; her son could *only* come through God's power.

God's promises are solely His responsibility to achieve; our only role is to *believe.*

Our belief steers every choice we make, so we must decide whose voice we heed. God asks us to trust in His words; Satan asks us to believe in circumstances. Either way, the heart of man will be captured.

A line from a movie speaks volumes to me and comes to mind often: "I think the answer...is to stop talking. Deny a voice to what's falling apart."[4] When we speak openly about problems, we give them a voice. In many words there is sin. We should only give voice to what supports our ability to believe God.

We have a say over whether or not disappointment takes root or remains rooted in our hearts. We can deny it a voice and any power over us, but we must be able to identify its manifestations. Disappointment seeds several attitudes, and each has a voice of its own. Let's take a closer look at some.

The voice of false hope

The voice of false hope is one of the devil's "favorites." This is not about having too much hope in a good thing. This is about hoping in the *wrong* thing.

To hope means to expect. Sarah operated in the false hope that Hagar and Abraham's collaboration was God's answer. Sarah intended to raise the child as her own. It was an interesting thought, but not a very practical one. Nor was it God's idea. His plan depended upon Abraham's *and* Sarah's faith to conceive.

Like any faithless voice, false hope must be confronted. It is a by-product of disappointment. Disappointment involves a reliance on our elementary nature and is a function of the flesh (our animalistic cravings). We take our eyes off God and His plan, and our lack of vision produces disappointment. From there we develop natural strategies to solve the problem, as Sarah did.

We are spirit beings made by God to live with intentional desires, not uncontrolled appetites such as disappointment and discouragement. In Christ we have the power to control them.

The voice of presumption and assumption

Sarah applied her faith to a solution she could readily understand. She was confident that Hagar could conceive and bring forth the promised child. This was the voice of presumption and assumption. To presume is to boldly take an idea for granted; to assume is to take something for granted without proof or to take responsibility (as in assuming a position).

Sarah presumed to know how the promise should come about. This led her to assume responsibility for making it happen. Do you see how different presumption is from faith? It is huge! Faith pleases God, but presumption is sinful perversion of faith. Sarah's intentions were good, but good intentions are no substitute for God's intentions. Wanting God's promises and love on our own terms is offensive to Him!

Like any sin, forcing the fulfillment of a promise misses the mark. It brings pleasure, but only momentarily. In the long run it is stressful. Stress then leads us to be selfishly motivated and inwardly focused. Then when things don't go our way, we are easily offended. Condemnation, rejection, and finally a spirit of Jezebel—the voice of rejection and low self-esteem manifested through pride—follow. When we distrust God's promise and exalt ourselves to perform it for Him we are acting just as Jezebel or Lucifer would.

You can see the lengths people go to avoid being disappointed—to the point of being thoroughly entangled in sin! The nagging voice of disappointment does not settle for disturbing us; it also stirs up strife and more offense.

Presumption and assumption are not God's voice.

THE TRICK OF FAMILIAR VOICES

Sometimes the voice vying for our attention is Satan's. Lucifer was created without sin. He eventually became corrupt, but *without* the help of a tempter. The Word calls him the father of lies (John 8:44).

Lucifer was made perfect, yet unrighteousness was found in him. He lied to himself and convinced himself that he was brilliant and self-sufficient. He forgot that he was created to worship God and not himself. Lucifer's vocation as the worshipping cherub was to bring the entire creation into God's presence. This mission was created in love and meant to be performed in love so all creation could experience God's love. But because Lucifer's heart became corrupted by self-love, he developed a deep hatred for God. That is when his vocation changed. No longer could he share God's love with the creation. Instead, Lucifer became a peddler of violence and rage. (See Ezekiel 28:14–16.)

Now Satan works to lead as many people as possible away from God. He craftily distracts them by his flattery and causes them to worship themselves, other people, the creation, and even himself. He cannot stand the perfection of God in those who were made in His image and likeness (a perfection coming only from God).

All the way back in the garden, Satan was infuriated by God's vast interest and investment in people. So he used a snake to lead humanity away from worshipping God. He did it by using Adam and Eve's own environment against them. He works the same way today: he uses our environment to introduce us to voices that contradict God's voice of goodness.

Disappointment is a big part of Satan's scheme. He used it in the garden when he said, "You won't die if you eat from this tree!" (See Genesis 3:4.) Do you hear the voice of disappointment? Satan wanted Adam and Eve to lose trust in the only trustworthy voice there is. Only God's voice could give them hope, faith, love, and the assurance of the goodness yet to come.

Thank God for the Second Adam, the Word of God who has given us the perfect light and life again. The key for us is to *not* think that we can sustain our own perfection. We cannot be perfect without Christ. Knowing this helps us avoid the traps Satan sets.

These traps are always familiar things we are inclined to readily accept. Think about it: if Satan introduced an entirely foreign object into your environment, you would resist it. But he uses things that are already in our hearts, according to James 1:14: "Instead, each person is tempted by his own desire, being lured and trapped by it" (ISV).

The enemy works to trap us with what is already inside us. Eve was trapped by the desire she had already considered. The enemy is conniving; he studies us in order to understand and identify our desires. Unfortunately most of these desires come from what we feel is missing in our lives. He uses these things to tempt us. We need to recognize this scheme, resist the devil, and kick him out of our environment just as God did. Christ has made us able to do so.

Familiar voices can keep us bound. For Sarah, everything was set in motion when she said, "Behold now, *the Lord has prevented me* from bearing children. Go in to my servant; it may be that I shall obtain children by her." (Gen. 16:2, ESV). The foundation of her belief was the voice of disappointment. It built in her heart a case for why her blessing had not yet come.

Disappointment always asks, "Why am I not receiving something good from God?" It manufactures unhealthy thoughts such as, "God is not true," "God doesn't do those good things," "God doesn't care," or "God does care, but not about me." These thoughts percolate when our predetermined expectations about *when, where,* and *how* differ from God's plan.

Without realizing it, we set our expectations based on what we think is right or normal. In Sarah's case, conceiving a child at age eighty was not normal. The idea that *she* would become pregnant seemed absurd.

Exactly! That's the perfect environment for God to perform miracles! You too may be waiting for something to be birthed beyond the "normal" time. It's never too late for God! When your natural abilities can no longer be trusted, God will manifest His supernatural ability and fulfill the promise—and no flesh will get the glory.

Very few people are willing to wait for such a miracle and keep hoping past the "reasonable" time of hoping. Those who believe they are looking out for our best interests will say, "Give up already! If it were going to happen, it would have already happened."

The problem is that people who say these things are not looking out for God's best interest. That is the mistake Peter made. He reprimanded Jesus when He announced that He was about to lay down His life. The idea seemed all wrong to Peter. Jesus responded sharply, saying, "Get behind Me, Satan! You are a hindrance to me for you mind the things of man and not the things of God." (See Matthew 16:23.)

The things of man make sense to mortal minds. The things of God are higher; they confound human reasoning. Jesus's rebuke of Peter might seem harsh, but Jesus recognized the voice of Satan in Peter's words. It was a familiar voice. Peter was speaking, but he expressed the ideas and ways of Satan.

Have you ever watched a ventriloquist work? At first you want to see whether his lips are moving. Then you think, "Wow he is good. I don't see his mouth moving at all." Little by little you become more focused on what the dummy is saying, and soon you are taken in by his personality. You laugh when he makes fun of the ventriloquist, because you see them as two different people.

Those are the tricks Satan plays! He does it *daily* to mislead God's chosen. The voice is powerful, not because of its force, but because it is familiar.

If we are to experience true and lasting joy, we must reject these false voices and tune in to God's.

Chapter 5

MASTER URGES AND EXPECTATIONS

S arah surrendered to voices that preyed upon her evalua-
tion of societal norms in respect to the time and space of
having a baby. No one else her age was believing to have a baby.
Sarah was well aware that her physical condition was not what
it used to be. She also realized that Hagar was in prime childbearing condition.

Perhaps Sarah overheard other women saying, "Can you
believe they are still believing for a child? How ridiculous!"

Environment and timing were casting their votes saying,
"Sarah, you are not the one God has chosen to give your husband a child." The pain of comparison with others generated
discontentment in Sarah's heart and the voice of reason hap-
pily chimed in.

In the same way that Satan made Eve think it wasn't normal
for God to know more than His people, Satan tries to tell us
what isn't normal. He wants us to believe that we are too old, too
young, too tall, too short, or too something else to receive the
promise. But God is not limited by natural factors.

Keep believing that your time, your child, your job, your healing are coming! Don't make comparisons that breed discontentment. I have found some of the most contented people in third world countries. They have no reference point that says life should be other than what it is. If I bring them to America or introduce them to a higher quality of life and then return them to their third world environment, discontentment often tempts them.

Our interpretation of our environment, norms, and expectations forms more of our personality than we realize. Children don't learn a poverty mind-set directly from lack. They learn about poverty from watching their parents deal with it. Statements such as "We can't afford to do (or buy) that" generate children's interpretations of lack. (It is worth noting that statements such as "We are saving to be able to do this or that" or "We will have to save and budget for that item," help children understand responsibility and priority, which are healthy values.)[1]

Comparison is Satan's staging ground for discontentment and disappointment, which in turn build unreasonable expectations. This is not about whether the reward is deserved, but about invalid reasons for wanting it. Unreasonable expectations lay a minefield of offense, resentment, jealousy, envy, and malice. When someone has what you want, you ask comparison questions: "How did you get that?" "How long did it take to build your company to that size?" "How many people come to your meetings?"

The implication is that if you reach the same goals at a slower rate or by different means, something is wrong; you are not as good or as talented or as smart or as powerful as they are. Then the question is: "What's wrong with me?"

Now disappointment has somewhere to live. From that point forward everything you see, hear, and think confirms your hidden fear: you are rejected, and God is preventing your dream from coming to pass.

That is where Sarah found herself. Her reasoning faculties kicked in and convinced her that God's plan could not be fulfilled through her. Because God had not filled in every detail of how the miracle would come, the devil helped to define a gray area that he could manipulate. From there he prodded Sarah to find her own solution.

In reality there was no gray area. There never is with God or His Word. There is no happenstance and there are no coincidences (there is no word for *coincidence* in the Hebrew language). With God, everything has a purpose and a specific means of development. Hagar had nothing to do with God's purpose, therefore His purpose would not be accomplished through Hagar. Nevertheless Sarah approached Abraham with her idea. This is when the power of Satan's voice becomes most evident: "Abram *listened* to the voice of Sarai" (Gen. 16:2, ESV).

Notice how Lucifer's resumé comes into play: he was given the power of divine influence on the heart. God's gifts are without repentance. When Satan's values changed, his gift didn't. He still influences the human heart. We say the battle is in the mind, but the spoil of the battle is the heart.

When Satan used the snake's body, he used his gift of influence. When Peter spoke to Christ, Satan used a voice to manipulate the heart. This is what he did with Sarah. He was able to do it because Sarah took her mind off the things of God and focused it on the things of man. Once that happened, Satan had his way.

MASTERS AND MASTERING URGES

If you yield your body to something, it becomes master of your body. Man is not really capable of self-mastery; he is built for submission to a master—either God or Satan. This is why the appetites of the flesh are dangerous; they are subject to an outside master. If God is the master of your flesh, you submit your appetites to Him and allow Him to choose what you will do. If the devil is the master of your flesh, then he calls the shots through uncontrolled appetites. He assesses your perceived needs and uses them to control your decision making.

Notice how Satan communicated with Eve in the garden. Play "the tape" in your head the way a boxer watches film of his opponent. Take note of Satan's strengths and weaknesses so you can overcome him and live in victory. Be aware of how he used small contextual changes to shift Eve away from God's ways.

God told Adam he could eat of any tree but one. Satan pulled a fast one on Eve by asking, "Has God indeed said, 'You shall not eat of *every* tree of the garden'?" (Gen. 3:1). He grossly exaggerated what God said, causing Eve to veer away from God's instruction. She said, "We may eat the fruit of the trees of the garden; but of the fruit of the tree which is in the midst of the garden, God has said, 'You shall not eat it, nor shall you touch it, lest you die'" (vv. 2–3).

God was very specific: "You must not eat fruit from a particular tree." Eve added the command not to touch it, but also diluted God's command to *not eat* the fruit. She quoted God as saying, "You shall not eat..." The difference is subtle but significant, and the enemy used it to his advantage.

Satan likes to make God's commands sound like suggestions. The Bible says that we shall eat of the good of the land—but wait— that's only true if we are willing and obedient (Isa. 1:19). There are necessary absolutes for those who walk with God. Obeying Him and His Word are absolutely required. The devil knows we like wiggle room, so he sells the benefits without the price or conditions that are attached.

God is light; Satan is darkness. God is good; the devil is bad. If we bend our lifestyles away from the biblical standard, we invite a mixture—a gray area. Satan likes that. The moment we move from "must" to "should" he is empowered to push the envelope.

With some prodding from the snake, bad fruit suddenly looked good to Eve. Rabbinical teaching says the devil also seized upon the phony detail about not touching the fruit by nudging Eve against the tree with his tail and saying, "See you touched it and you didn't die! Now why don't you go ahead and taste it? It will illuminate you with wisdom."

Can you see why the Bible is so clear about not adding to or subtracting from the Word of God? (See Deuteronomy 4:2.) The devil will use it against us every time.

He also uses his influence to mess with divine timing. Eve had obeyed God's command not to eat from the forbidden tree until Satan manipulated her natural urges and made eating the bad fruit seem urgent. This should speak to us: decisions made in haste or with the emotion of urgency are rarely produced by God.

Urges are not always wrong or sinful. The urge to drink water is designed to quench thirst. The urge to do a good job is necessary for success. Compassion is an urge that moves us to help others. The anointing or unction is an urge that empowers us to change lives. Peace and patience are also urges from God.

But when improper urges take over, a sense of desperation prompts us to act unwisely, leading to disappointment. There was no real urgency for Sarah to produce a child, but comparisons and manipulated expectations created a sense of urgency that prompted a bad decision. Outside pressure forced internal anxiety and desperation. Sarah was overwhelmed with pressures she could not process internally. This produced great stress and the natural desire to act in ways that relieved the pressure.

Some people smoke to get this kind of relief. Others drink. Some become restless and hyperactive. None of these approaches are beneficial. The best response is prayer. Studies of the brain show that prayer is a great stress reliever.[2] But prayer is too rarely our first urge.

I repeat: experiencing urges is not evil. Failing to subject them to the master is where the trouble starts. However, when we humble ourselves and lay our urges before Him, all of the fruit of the Spirit are manifested, and our urges and emotions are properly managed.

URGE MASTERY: TORAH IN US

God gave Israel His Torah to help them manage and train their urges. Paul refers to Torah as a schoolmaster (Gal. 3:24–25)—not a teacher waiting to spank us, but one that reveals the sweetness and benefit of God's Word, which is not given as punishment but from His goodness.

God discipled Abram, and he became a new man named Abraham. God's original work with Adam in the garden continued with Abraham. God proved that He could elevate man's stature; even though he was fallen, he could be made righteous through God's faith—if he was both willing and obedient.

As Abraham walked before God, God watched his lifestyle and made him our example of righteousness by faith. From Abraham's example God dictated the standards and principles which we call *the Law* (more correctly, principles or teaching). The intention of the Torah, the spirit of the Law, was not to control man (as it later did under corrupt leadership), but to help man recognize and resist every offer from the tree of the knowledge of good and evil.

The psalmist wrote: "I hate the double-minded, but I love your law" (Ps. 119:113). Why? The law was designed to keep us on track through guidance, not control. Through Jesus we have the same Law, but now it is written on our hearts and minds, and urged through the inspiration of the Holy Spirit. We have been empowered by God's grace to keep His principles for successful living. In being Spirit led, we can walk in the God-likeness of Adam and the godliness of Abraham. We do it all through the sonship made available to us through Jesus.

The fruit of the Spirit is the fruit of righteousness. Love, peace, joy, longsuffering, and so forth are managed urges brought under control within the human soul. We cannot have uncontrolled emotions and be righteous. Uncontrolled emotions lead to uncontrolled behavior, which leads to uncontrolled living and patterns tending to destruction.

Controlled emotions do the opposite: they become highways to successful living. We must, however, understand the limits of our control. We use terms such as *time management* as though we had some power over time. We are in no way able to manage time. The best we can do is manage ourselves within an environment and a timeline. (When we feel stressed out, we can manage our emotions and blow off steam by exercising, praying, walking barefoot in the park, or doing all three at once!) That is self-management, which is the management of our emotions. There will always be time and space issues that we cannot control. Our job is to focus on what we *can* control, which is us. When we do that, we maintain the culture of Abraham, who believed God and had it accounted to him as righteousness (Rom. 4:20–22).

Rationalization was not part of Abraham's lifestyle, and it should not be part of ours. God never intended for time or environment or other people to take our focus off Him. When our focus drifts, we attempt to justify and explain ourselves logically. This is rationalization. We try to support our opinions, excuses, and actions with input from people, places, and other sources of information. In other words, we borrow a play from Satan's book: we use our environment to justify what's going on inside us.

This is the devil's way, and it is contrary to God's intent for us. God ordained that the internal would control the external, not the other way around. You have probably heard the analogy of the thermostat and the thermometer. The thermostat is an internal mechanism that controls the environment; the thermometer reacts to the environment.

God's Word and promises are the internal controls designed to dictate our interactions with the environment. This type of living doesn't adhere to a list of what is good and bad. Instead, it causes us to eat *only* from the tree of life which is devoid of the knowledge of evil. When we eat of the tree of life, we can see that all things work together for good (Rom. 8:28). We find good in everything and we thank God in every circumstance. We are not celebrating good and bad as equals, but trusting God's involvement more than we trust the circumstances before our eyes.

The difference between God-inspired urges and Satan-inspired urges should be clear. We are not thermometers, but thermostats! Satan must never be allowed to pressure us into emotion-based decision making. His voice of condemnation and confusion should always be drowned out by God's voice of edification, exhortation, and comfort (1 Cor. 14:3). The devil comes to steal, kill, and destroy, but Jesus came to give unto us life more abundantly (John 10:10).

My goal is to expose the enemy and remove his covering. We are not to be ignorant of his devices (2 Cor. 2:11). When we are wise to his strategies, which are not spiritual but carnal, we will walk in complete victory. We overcome demonic powers and live in the Spirit through God's revelation of Himself.

Finally there is no power struggle between God and the devil or between God's kingdom and the realms of darkness. God is victorious, and Satan is defeated. God is with us! We agree with Him and His Word, and they dictate our interaction with people and environments.

The greater our agreement with Him, the greater our victory in life. As long as we listen to God's voice and His voice only, we will live His promises!

Chapter 6

TAKE A LICKIN' AND KEEP ON TICKIN'

W hat makes a person lose heart? Usually it is disappointment—something the person believed would happen did not happen in the manner or timing expected. Even if the expectation was accurate, the plan seemed washed up if the timeline was off.

When expectation and timing fail to align, disappointment follows. This is what happened to Sarah. She was right to expect a miracle child, but her timing was wrong. "So, after Abram had lived ten years in the land of Canaan, Sarai, Abram's wife, took Hagar the Egyptian, her servant, and gave her to Abram her husband as a wife" (Gen. 16:3, ESV). In her disappointment, Sarah took matters into her own hands.

Along with timing and expectation, temptation plays a role in disappointment. My wife has a saying: "Circumstances are subject to change." The prefix, *circum* is used in many words, including *circumference*. The prefix means "round about, around…to encompass or surround *(circumference; circumjacent; circumstance)* or to go around."[1]

By definition our circumstances surround us. Our surroundings influence and tempt us. Taken at face value, they can dis-
hearten us. They don't have to! To use my wife's saying: "Whatever
is encompassing or surrounding us is subject to change."

When our surroundings dictate how we live and feel, we are
overwhelmed, but when change begins in us, it also comes to our
surroundings. We are usually tempted to try the reverse strategy:
when disappointed we try changing the timing or the surroundings in order to change how we feel. This brings temporary relief
because it simulates progress. Ultimately, however, it produces
greater despair. And unless we admit our error, we work just as
hard to rationalize why we were doomed from the start.

People in this state of mind often decide that God is not good.
They accuse Him of rejecting them or they blame other people
for their misery. This is a trap!

I have fallen into some traps of my own. Often when the
freeway gets backed up, the thought of zooming down a side
road flashes in my mind. So I exit the highway, only to get
stuck at a light. Pretty soon there's another light. From the side
road I can see the freeway traffic moving faster than I am. My
"fix" failed!

Why do we do this? It is because we like activity more than
waiting. Our impatience and foolishness trick us into thinking
we are actually accomplishing something when in actuality we
are bogging down the plan.

If we would just stay on the freeway, turn on some music,
and enjoy the ride we would arrive at our destination just as
quickly, better rested, and with more peace. We are so focused
on time...time...hurry...hurry...hurry. But the kingdom of
God is not about rushing or eating or drinking. The kingdom
of God is "righteousness and peace and joy in the Holy Spirit"
(Rom. 14:17). Our shortcuts sometimes save us time but at the
cost of these benefits.

KINGDOM WAITING

Trust, rest, and wait have different meanings in the world than they do in the kingdom. From an earthly perspective I trust what I see. In the kingdom I trust what I don't see. In the world I rest when I am in control. In the kingdom I rest in the Lord. In the world I wait only when I have no other choice. In the kingdom I wait on God's instruction, leading, and guidance because I recognize the benefits of doing so.

Once when I was grocery shopping I needed to use the restroom. As I approached it, I found a worker leaning against the wall, waiting for everyone to leave the restroom so she could clean it. With her head in her hands and looking weary and irritated, she slid down the wall.

I asked, "Are you waiting patiently?"

She replied with a lifeless "yes."

Walking past her I realized that she *believed* she was being patient, but her posture and tone of voice told a different story. She *was* waiting, but patience was not involved.

We tend to think that if time is passing and we are standing still, then we are waiting patiently. The Hebrew word for waiting is *qavah*. It means "to bind together (perhaps by twisting), i.e, collect; (figuratively) to expect…gather (together), look, patiently, tarry, wait (for, on, upon)."[2]

When God is involved in your dream, your waiting is fruitful. He works to bind you, the dream, and Himself together, like three cords twisted together to become an inseparable and unbreakable rope. As Solomon wrote: "Though one may be overpowered by another, two can withstand him. And a threefold cord is not quickly broken" (Eccles. 4:12).

In the kingdom dynamic waiting changes something in us before it changes what is around us. We should be growing through the power of the Spirit as we become more and more connected, reliant, and supported by Him. Instead, we are tempted to see *self* as our greatest ally.

God would prefer to have that place in our lives. That is why most of our waiting seems designed to destroy our reliance on our own ability, talents, and skills. The Word calls our trust in those abilities *the flesh*. God will use our gifts, but He wants to be involved. Then He can support and supply us with strength, courage, patience, and joy.

The Bible says, "Wait on the LORD; be of good courage, and He shall strengthen your heart; wait, I say, on the LORD!" (Ps. 27:14). As we wait, God becomes our strength. We develop the courage and strength necessary to possess the desired thing *and* to keep it.

This is where lottery winners get in trouble. Because it takes no time or commitment to *earn* the million dollars, they never learn to wait, and they never develop the courage and strength needed to hold on to their winnings.

When we bypass the painful and formative process of waiting, we lack the tools to sustain our gains. The most important aspect of waiting is not getting the prize, but gaining strength in the process, as Isaiah explained: "But those who *wait on the Lord* shall renew their strength; they shall mount up with wings like eagles, they shall run and not be weary, they shall walk and not faint" (Isa. 40:31). Notice that the key is not in waiting for the desired end, but in waiting on the Lord.

For example, a woman waiting to have a baby has a different focus from a woman who is waiting on the Lord to bless her with a baby. Both women have babies in mind, but the first one is waiting for a change in circumstances. The posture of the second woman is inclined not only to the gift, but also toward God's purpose in giving it.

If God is our supply, He understands the level of courage and strength needed to raise a healthy child in the environment in which we live. We can trust Him for the right timing—and the waiting will only confirm that He *is* our supplier. He will cause

us to mount up with wings like eagles, much as adult eagles do
for their young:

> Bald eagle babies attempt to fly between 10 and 13 weeks
> of age. As described in *An Eagle to the Sky,* Frances
> Hamerstrom documents her observations of one eaglet's
> parent beginning a phase of passing over the nest repeat-
> edly without food, unlike ever before. Over time the
> eaglet began to lose weight, but also became lighter and
> quicker in its movements. In time it became airborne, if
> for only a few moments at a time, in its attempts to reach
> the circling parent.
>
> As the eaglet continued to struggle to reach upward,
> its strength progressively increased to the point where the
> parent would begin passing over the nest with food once
> again. Further encouraging the young little bird's desire,
> the eaglet eventually hopped out of the nest thus taking
> its first flight. Coasting on a current of wind it glided
> across the valley and toppled onto land. Still hungry but
> unhurt, the effort was rewarded as the parent dropped
> the enticing food to the eaglet as a hard-earned prize.[3]

The Lord trains us in similar ways. He sets a joy before us so
we become willing to gain the strength to fly. Once our strength
is increased, we can soar. As the eagle uses food to draw its
young into flight, God uses our desired result to get us moving
forward. He could easily give us the desire, but as weak, flight-
less, nest-bound creatures we would not be fit to handle it.

Too often, instead of tying ourselves to God and waiting for
Him to perform His promises, we wait for circumstances to
change. Scripture says: "Delayed hope makes one sick at heart,
but a *fulfilled longing is a tree of life*" (Prov. 13:12, GW). When
our perspective is off, we focus on what looks like delay. But God
wants excitement and expectation in Him to guide us toward the
longing fulfilled! After years of waiting, Sarah realized she was

infertile and unable to produce the promise. That was the point! God's promise is of the Spirit. It does not and *cannot* come from the flesh, even when it must come *through* the flesh. Jesus performed the greatest work ever done in humankind, and it came *through* the flesh. Yet it was completely from the Spirit, as though coming through a veil into the natural realm.

How long will it take us to realize that it is not by might, nor by power, but by the Spirit? (See Zechariah 4:6.) Sarah and Abraham's ability to conceive the promised child seemed normal enough, but it was never meant to be common. No flesh can glory in the promise fulfilled by God. How long did it take for Sarah's heart to get sick of trusting in her ability and in the knowledge of good and evil?

How long will it take us?

We have opportunities to choose the tree of life over the tree of the knowledge of good and evil. Will we surrender our flesh? Will we realize (as Sarah finally did) that our skills, abilities, and talents can only fall short? Will we settle for natural things when God offers eternal things that are so much bigger, better, and more sure?

I know you don't want to settle. But do you feel as Sarah did that you are the reason your promise has not yet come to pass?

In the bigger picture you are right. That is what makes the reward a bigger miracle! You can't add to it, nor take the glory for it. If you don't think you need a miracle, then you will trust in your flesh. You will believe in what you know about the world and about other people's experiences in getting what you want.

Abraham and Sarah were blessed on every side except for the one thing that would confirm God's promise that many nations would come from them. The confirmation they wanted was a child—just *one* child—and Sarah was unable to produce it! It was absolutely necessary that her self-reliance hit the wall. This must have hurt her most, especially because she could not do what other women did with ease. Imagine how their opinions weighed upon her!

Other people's opinions only matter when we are caught up in the flesh. This distorts our vision and tempts us to grow weary in waiting simply because our hope is delayed. Remember: "Delayed hope makes one sick at heart, but a *fulfilled longing is a tree of life*" (Prov. 13:12, GW).

We need to know what delayed hope is. Hope is fairly straightforward: it's expectation. The word translated "delayed" is the Hebrew word *mashak,* defined by Strong's as follows:

> To draw, used in a great variety of applications (including to sow, to sound, to prolong, to develop, to march, to remove, to delay, to be tall, etc.)...draw (along, out), continue, defer, extend, forbear, give, handle, make...long, sow, scatter, stretch out.[4]

We should never move away from God being our source. Once the source changes, our expectation is drawn away. Then it is only a matter of time before disappointment sickens the heart.

"MEDITAINMENT"

Think about it: If God wants to tie Himself and His Word of promise to our hearts, shouldn't that become our focus in waiting? Of course it should! One morning as I prayed, a made-up word popped into my mind. I had never thought of or heard it before, so I knew that it was inspired. It was the word *meditainment.*

I know! It's not a real word. But it does have meaning. In fact, it opens a revelation: we are always meditating on something. Most of the time we prefer to focus on what is interesting or entertaining—*meditainment.* Our meditation should be on God, His Word, His promise, and the fact that He is our source for everything. When we make those issues our focus, then we will have prosperity and success.

Do you remember God's words to Joshua when he assumed the leadership of Israel after Moses's death?

> This Book of the Law shall not depart from your mouth, but you shall meditate in it day and night, that you may observe to do according to all that is written in it. For then you will make your way prosperous, and then you will have good success.
>
> —JOSHUA 1:8

In verse 7 of the same chapter God told Joshua not to turn to the left or the right. His meditation was to be on God's Word day and night. Joshua obeyed; his way was *made* prosperous, and he was *made* to have good success. God made things happen for Joshua as long as he saw God as his source.

The same thing happens for you and me if we meditate on God's Word and provision. God will *make* us prosperous and successful in good ways. Remember that whatever we meditate on controls our expectations. We are entertained by what we meditate on. Entertainment is the process of occupying the mind. It's a diversion. Meditainment happens when your meditation is diverted and occupied with circumstances, for example. When your mind becomes occupied with circumstances instead of the person who can change the circumstances, that's meditainment.

The shift in thinking is small. I'm not saying you shouldn't dream of having that child or of being a world changer through ministry, business, or parenting. I am saying that when you dream, your meditation should revolve around your relationship with God. When you believe for something from Him, you should become more and more dependent on Him, not less. Instead of being entertained by circumstances, be occupied with Him.

That is what Joseph did when the manifestation of his dream seemed to stall. "Until the time that his word came to pass, the word of the LORD tested him" (Ps. 105:19). Joseph had to decide what he would allow to occupy his mind. He chose well and received his reward.

Whatever you meditate on causes your reticular activating system (RAS) to kick in. RAS is God's gift to keep us focused and on task. When we meditate over and over again on certain outcomes, the RAS function in the brain isolates relevant information. Everything related to the desired outcome is highlighted and everything unrelated is moved aside.

Of course, we can become very focused on the wrong thing, and the RAS will still kick in. So if our meditation excludes God as our source and all we want is the promise fulfilled, our expectation and focus will be elevated, but we will seek resolution at any cost. This method of achievement is exhausting, and can ultimately cause us to lose hope.

In reality hope is never really lost. It can be distracted or even delayed. It can also be perverted. Fear is perverted hope that has forgotten God as our source. We know fear is not from God, because He hasn't given us fear, but love, power, and a stable mind (2 Tim. 1:7). If our meditation leads us away from these qualities, we can be sure that God is *not* leading our expectation. Instead, we have been drawn away. The pressure of our circumstances might be temporarily eased, but the distraction will ultimately lead to a dead end.

HOPE, FAITH, PATIENCE, AND OBEDIENCE

Hope for the believer is integrally tied to faith. "Now faith is the substance of things hoped for, the evidence of things not seen" (Heb. 11:1). When circumstances are drawn out longer than expected, we are tempted to lose hope. But faith is the foundation of hope. When hope is lost, it is impossible to have faith, and without faith it is impossible to please God (Heb. 11:6). To outlast the negative effects of circumstances, we must sustain hope for the duration or faith will be short-lived.

Hope and faith run on a timeline. It takes time for your expectation to be drawn away. It also takes time for your promise to come to pass and for God to complete His perfect work in you. God's partner in this work is patience, which works on the same timeline with hope and faith. Allow patience to do its perfecting work in you no matter how terrible your circumstances seem.

If patience has more work to do, but your hope has been exhausted, you will grow weary and sick of waiting, forgetting that you must trust only God as your source. Obedience is key in this. Other methods and sources will not sustain you for the long haul.

When God is your source, obedience gives you access to His reserves. Only He knows the secret of success, but He is unwilling to share it with those who refuse His ways. If you are willing and obedient you will eat the good of the land (Isa. 1:19).

The sicker people's hearts become, the less willing and obedient they will be. I am not saying they intentionally become more rebellious. I am saying they become increasingly dull to the truth of what real change demands of them. They can end up believing the world's ideas: "I deserve to be happy" or "I have to do what feels right" or "God is gracious and He will forgive me if I make a mistake."

God *is* gracious. He makes His will known to us so we can be willing and obedient. But when our hearts are sick, our willpower dwindles and we cannot obey Him.

Heart issues are crucial. The Hebrew word for heart is *lev,* essentially two letters, LV. It refers to the bedrock of all emotions. When God asks us to LoVe Him with all of our LV, He wants us to give Him our emotions. Even more than that, He wants us to let Him lead our emotions so they can't lead us.

My wife says that emotions are not designed to be leaders but followers. She is right. We often make unstable decisions because we are driven by emotions. If we gave God our LV, we would not make emotional decisions, only willing and obedient ones.

This requires that we love and trust God more than anything or anyone else. We have to believe that He wants us to be happy more than we want to be happy. He is the only one who knows what will make us happy anyway!

In the wilderness the children of Israel insistently asked God for something He did not want them to have. The Bible says God gave them their request and with it came leanness, or thinness, in their souls (Ps. 106:15). Having their way over God's way produced a shallow willpower and the inability to make right decisions. Leanness is also the inability to keep commitments and recognize right from wrong. Leanness shortens our faith and produces a sick heart.

Picture the jeans worn by a crawling child. The repeated friction on the knees wears the fabric thin until it loses strength and integrity. This is what happens when we demand something other than God's best. The leanness of our souls turns our perspective and prayers from what pleases God to what pleases us. Our stubbornness might get us what we want, but disappointment will come with it.

In His goodness He gave His Holy Spirit to teach and lead us—and even to pray for us when we don't know how (Rom. 8:26). But if we refuse to give the Holy Spirit leadership over our hearts, He cannot keep our souls from being sick.

SPEARHEADS AND SUFFERING

Waiting can be frustrating, but it doesn't have to be. We must understand why God sometimes sees fit to keep us on a timeline that seems to deny progress. Notice I said "seems." What we perceive is based upon our expectation, the spearhead of every endeavor. Negative expectation is the spearhead of defeat. The expectation of good things spearheads victory.

Even with the right spearhead, waiting tests us. Hope plays a critical role as we have seen, and we ought to rejoice in that. But

Scripture tells us to rejoice even more over another prime ingredient of waiting: suffering.

> We have also obtained access by faith into this grace
> in which we stand, and we rejoice in hope of the glory
> of God. Not only that, but we rejoice in our sufferings,
> knowing that suffering produces endurance, and endur
> ance produces character, and character produces hope.
> —Romans 5:2–4, esv

Paul said suffering produces endurance, which produces character. Character is needed if we are to keep the promises that God fulfills. Character then produces hope, which is the understanding that God would never leave or forsake us. Hope waits, and waiting makes us more like God. How else can we outlast the storms and hold on to our dreams?

We have seen how disappointment causes setbacks. Endurance, character, and hope help to lift us above disappointment. Suffering plays a part. Often waiting *is* suffering. Sarah suffered when all hope of bearing a child seemed lost. She assumed that God missed the baby appointment, so she was disappointed.

Some say disappointment is really a missed appointment. Sarah's story proves that God never misses His appointments. He is faithful, true, integrous, and loving—in other words, totally dependable!

God kept His word to Sarah. What God says, He does. He kept His appointment, and Sarah was rewarded for her faith, even though she struggled along the way. She was disappointed not because of a missed appointment, but by what she saw as a broken promise. This is what disappoints people: the sense that a promise, covenant, or vow has been broken.

We must beware of this pattern in our own lives. We often miss God opportunities because offense leaves us distracted, discontented, discouraged, discombobulated, disoriented, or disunited. Our focus on God as provider is broken and we focus on "dis-" we have suffered.

This pattern is discontinued when we turn to Jesus, who is the author and finisher of our faith (Heb. 12:2). When we fix our eyes on Him, "fulfilled longing is a tree of life" (Prov. 13:12, GW). Ancient Jewish wisdom says the tree of life is the source of infinite life. The Midrash refers to the Torah as the tree of life. Jesus is the living Torah—the way, the truth, and the life (John 14:6). Expectation produces life!

At some point, however, we must accept suffering as part of the waiting experience. Then if we continue without giving up, the promise will be fulfilled. If we use it, our faith is strong enough to push us beyond obstacles and road bumps. We need to maintain a "whatever it takes" attitude, and we will gain a second wind to carry us over the finish line.

The finish line is a good place, because fulfillment of godly desires is a tree of life. The Hebrew word translated "fulfilled" has several applications, including "to go or come…abide, apply, attain."[5] The Hebrew word for "longing" is *ta'avah*. It is "a longing; by implication, a delight (subjectively, satisfaction, objectively a charm)."[6]

The definition of *longing* is important. The English word means "strong, persistent desire or craving, especially for something unattainable or distant…having or characterized by persistent or earnest desire."[7]

Let's learn how to maintain our longing by blending our definitions of *longing* and *fulfilled:*

- Longing to keep going—don't give up or quit hoping!

- Longing to come back—don't stop expecting resurgence and restitution. Keep looking for it.

- Longing to abide—don't stop dwelling on the promise.

- Longing applied—don't stop applying the promise
  to every circumstance.

- Longing attained—pursue as if you already have it.

One of the arts of never being bored in waiting is to make sure you have something to work toward. If you are "longing forward," expecting good things to come, dwelling on the good things already attained, applying the good to your future, and walking as if you already have what you have asked for, then you can avoid falling into disappointment and despair.

Have you ever owned a Timex? Timex watches were long advertised to "take a lickin' and keep on tickin'." I saw an old commercial in which a Timex was tied to the propeller of a motorboat and submerged. When the engine started, the propeller turned at forty-five hundred revolutions per minute. At the end of the commercial, the watch still worked.

You are like that Timex! You can handle everything that comes your way and keep on tickin'. Just keep the timing of the Lord and you will never lose time or miss an opportunity. Maintain your expectation, and you will have the tree of life.

Trees never produce just once; they keep yielding fruit season after season. When God's promise is manifested, your experience in faith, hope, and patience will continue to produce. But you must keep your heart focused on the right things. Paul the apostle encouraged the Philippian church to meditate on anything noble, joyous, virtuous, or of spiritual value (Phil. 4:8). He said this knowing that when promises are fulfilled, they testify to God's past goodness and they prophesy good things to come. If God did it before, He will do it again. If He did it for someone else, then for sure He can and will do it for you and me.

Our lives should be the garden of God, planted with many trees of life. When we willingly obey and are unwilling to quit, we will eat of the good of the land many times over.

Chapter 7

CHOOSE HAPPINESS

Τ he first thing God spoke to Adam and Eve was a blessing
that was designed to guide them through a life of victory:

> God blessed them, and God said to them, "Be fruitful and
> multiply; fill the earth and subdue it; have dominion over
> the fish of the sea, over the birds of the air, and over every
> living thing that moves on the earth."
> —GENESIS 1:28

I believe God's desire is the same today as it was in the garden—
to benefit His people. In Psalm 1:1–2 we discover the key to King
David's posture toward life.

> Blessed is the man who walks not in the counsel of the
> wicked, nor stands in the way of sinners, nor sits in the
> seat of scoffers; but his delight is in the law of the LORD,
> and on his law he meditates day and night.
> —ESV

According to this verse King David consistently did three
things: he watched how he walked; he chose who he would stand

with; and he was careful about where he sat. If we do these things, the blessing will flow unhindered in our lives too.

Godly conduct leads to blessing. The Hebrew word for blessed means "happiness" as *The Amplified Bible* shows:

> Blessed (happy, fortunate, prosperous, and enviable) is the man who walks and lives not in the counsel of the ungodly [following their advice, their plans and purposes], nor stands [submissive and inactive] in the path where sinners walk, nor sits down [to relax and rest] where the scornful [and the mockers] gather.
>
> —PSALM 1:1–2, AMP

God desires His people to be blessed. People often say, "I have a right to be happy." Unfortunately they often say it when justifying their ungodly decisions. Yes, we all should be happy, but not through unhealthy methods or schemes. So let's examine more closely the psalmist's three ways to guarantee happiness.

WICKED COUNSEL

In his book *Outwitting the Devil* Napoleon Hill explains that disappointment is a course correction for stubbornness.[1] With that in mind let's discuss the counsel of the wicked.

The way of the wicked is a perverted one, because the wicked intentionally resist the knowledge of God. These are people who know the difference between right and wrong, but they choose to do wrong anyway.

The word *wicked* in Psalm 1:1 means "morally wrong; concretely an (actively) bad person."[2] It is impossible to be happy and moving forward in life when you take advice from bad people. How can you expect good, long-lasting fruit when you take advice from those who have set themselves against God and His Word and fail to recognize His existence?

You cannot!

THE WAY OF SINNERS

The psalmist's second admonition is to avoid standing in the way of sinners. This pictures the progression of evils. You start by walking in the counsel of the wicked, which makes you inclined to stand in their ways. First, you listen with intrigue to their ideas. It then becomes easier to imitate their actions. The progression of sin continues according to the level of your tolerance.

Bad company will always corrupt good morals (1 Cor. 15:33). This is at the heart of the psalmist's warning to stay away, *if* you want to be happy.

THE SCOFFER'S SEAT

The more comfortable you become frequenting the way of sinners, the easier it is to sit down and partake of their scorn, ridicule, and insulting humor. What used to be offensive now seems acceptable, so you make excuses for it.

God gave us the gift of laughter to build community and harmony. Instead, humor is often used to separate and divide. Only human beings can laugh. Happy people cannot feel comfortable around improper humor.

The psalmist is not against laughter, but against things that should not be laughed at. Scorners base their humor on prejudices, sacrilege, and unclean suggestions. The scorners feel included by excluding and demeaning others. The wicked, sinners, and scoffers build up their own emotions by breaking down the emotions of their victims.

Let us never slump to the scorner's level or stand in the pompous place of sinners or walk in the waywardness of the wicked!

The apostle Paul took the psalmist's thoughts about godly living further, writing: "See then that you walk circumspectly, not as fools but as wise, redeeming the time, because the days are evil" (Eph. 5:15–16). When we say no to foolishness, we redeem what has been lost over time, and wisdom becomes available to us.

DELIGHTING IN GOD'S WAYS

Let's get back to Sarah. I know what you are thinking: "What does Psalm 1 have to do with her? She was neither wicked, nor a sinner, nor scornful."

You are absolutely right. The first psalm goes on to say, "His delight is in the law of the LORD, and on his law he meditates day and night" (Ps. 1:2, ESV). The Torah was given to Moses, not Abraham. Abraham and Sarah walked before God by faith and not through the written or oral Torah.

Those who live by faith do not live in sin. But those who do things not based upon faith are in sin. Although Sarah did not intentionally lead Abraham astray, he was still led away from God's best, which involved not just Abraham and *his* seed, but also Sarah. Their line would be a blessing to the whole earth!

When we delight and meditate on God's principles, all other advice is inferior. It might not be wicked advice, but it is not from God and should not be acted upon. For example, according to the Tehillim commentary on Psalm 1:1-2, Jewish believers should never receive counsel from those who do not study the Torah.[3] Advice that doesn't come from the principles of God is from the way of the wicked, the sinner, and the scorner.

Sarah was none of the above. Nor did she have a Bible to consult. Yet, God had given the promise and was able to give further instructions on how to achieve it.

When you and I make decisions without considering God's righteous guidance, we should not be surprised when disappointment follows. Consulting God after we have decided, asked other people, searched other sources, and watched our plans go awry is not what is meant by delighting in God's principles. Scripture says: "Without counsel plans fail, but with many advisers they succeed" (Prov. 15:22, ESV). The King James Version reads: "Without counsel purposes are disappointed: but in the multitude of counsellors they are established." This is true, but many counselors should never take the place of the first counselor, which is the Word of God.

Happy men and women do not make decisions based upon presumption or assumption, but assurance *only.* Only the Word of God can assure a blessed life. Search the Word for answers. Delight in His principles and seek to do His will. Walk differently from the wicked because their standards are completely different. The blessed man's seat is a seat of authority and dominion, not scorn. Jokers and fools tear down others and make up their own minds about how to live. The wise build up others and allow God to make up their mind for them.

God's will and man's will are not the same. God's ways and thoughts are higher than ours. We can lie, but God cannot (Num. 23:19); it is opposite to His nature and character. He is completely trustworthy. Once we grasp this truth, we have a greater chance of living faith-filled lives.

With lingering doubts about God's perfect love and absolute goodness, we are left to believe the circumstances and live in presumption. King Saul made that mistake, and Samuel rebuked him, saying: "Rebellion is as the sin of divination, and presumption is as iniquity and idolatry. Because you have rejected the word of the LORD, he has also rejected you from being king" (1 Sam. 15:23, ESV).

If we believe God is not good, faithful, or loving, we align ourselves with the fools described below:

> The fool says in his heart, "There is no God." They are corrupt, they do abominable deeds, there is none who does good. The LORD looks down from heaven on the children of man, to see if there are any who understand, who seek after God.
> —PSALM 14:1–2, ESV

Because they believe they are right, fools allow what is in their hearts to direct their steps. Their thinking is diametrically opposed to God's ways. The righteous never trust their flesh. They trust only God's Word and Spirit. They know that those who allow their own hearts to lead will always choose what is emotionally pleasing. They choose God's way instead; the mind of the spirit within them believes the Word and informs the heart of God's truth. Their bodies then willingly obey.

When people are convinced that they are right, there is no room in their hearts for another truth. Truth needs a vacancy to occupy. Often we must unlearn in order to relearn. But first we must realize that we don't know the truth.

So how do we become blind to the truth? Offense can cause blind spots. Real hurts can prevent us from learning. We often resist dealing with our painful experiences, so we reject new information. It is a futile attempt to keep the "scab" on our wounds.

This is exactly what Sarah did. Her situation was painful, so she buried it under her own plan:

> And *Sarai said to Abram,* "Behold now, the LORD has prevented me from bearing children. *Go in to my servant;* it may be that I shall obtain children by her." And *Abram listened to the voice of Sarai.*
> —GENESIS 16:2, ESV

Just because the person advising you is a godly person doesn't mean that they are giving you godly counsel. Unless a person is speaking the Word and principles of God, it is not His counsel. Sarah formed an opinion within her own mind and gave it to Abraham as advice. But her idea was not based upon God's favor; it was based upon her own disappointment, as her words reveal: "The LORD has prevented me..."

Sarah's opinion was incorrect, therefore her counsel was wrong and could only lead to wrong actions. No person's counsel should ever be elevated above God's Word. Only by choosing His Word above all else can His blessing be released.

My own life proves this true. The loss of my grandfather was so devastating to me that I could not believe God was real. If He was real why would He allow me to experience so much pain? I assumed that He either didn't care, wasn't powerful enough to spare me from suffering, or wasn't real.

My theories left no room for any other truth.

It is impossible to both believe and be offended. Offense comes when we stop believing that someone loves us, believes in us, or can be trusted. Offense and disappointment are close relatives. Unbelief is a form of offense. It comes when your understanding runs out. Disappointment happens when your faith tank is in overdraft. Ultimately it will lead to shipwrecked faith, as Paul the apostle explained: "Holding faith, and a good conscience; which some having put away concerning faith have made shipwreck" (1 Tim. 1:19, KJV).

To be shipwrecked means to be stranded and void of navigation. When you are shipwrecked you feel like all direction, confidence, and guidance are lost. According to Paul, losing faith and a good conscience is as good as being shipwrecked. That means they are priceless, as we will see.

King David said, "The steps of a good man are ordered *by the Lord*, and He delights in his way" (Ps. 37:23). God is good, and we are made in His image and likeness. But we were not trained to walk in our true identity as God's sons until Jesus came. God sent Him to pre-walk our steps. All we have to do is follow Christ, and we will not fulfill the lust of the flesh.

When I read about the good man's steps being ordered by the Lord, I picture Christ walking ahead and leaving tracks for me to follow. As I walk circumspectly, led by the Spirit, I step into each track that Jesus prepared before the foundations of the world.

This reminds me that Jesus is my High Priest (Heb. 2:17). Like Aaron, He has anointing oil running down His beard and His garment and into His footsteps (Ps. 133), leaving puddles of anointing oil for me to walk in. As I carefully step into each footprint, oil covers my ankles and then my knees, until it reaches the top of my head.

This is where the blessing is commanded! The Lord has commanded a life of blessing for us to enjoy. If you have not yet enjoyed it, open your mind to His goodness and step into the way of the master. You were guided, ordered, and anointed to walk as a happy man and woman of God. Even when your circumstances seem contrary, *you are blessed!*

Chapter 8

NAVIGATING THE STORMS OF LIFE

More often than not we are our own worst enemies. When disappointment brings sin, guilt, and depression, self-sabotage and shipwrecked faith threaten our well-being. When we take too little responsibility, excuse-making and a seared conscience follow.

Whatever challenges we face, we have to navigate! A teaching from the Talmud says the world is like an ocean, with rough and tumultuous waters. Faith in God is the boat, and the Word of God is the anchor that keeps the boat from being tossed to and fro in rough seas.

We see the same line of thinking from the apostle Paul, including in a scripture already discussed in which Paul urged Timothy to keep "holding faith and a good conscience. By rejecting this, some have made shipwreck of their faith" (1 Tim. 1:19, ESV).

Holding faith is not a simple term or a passive application. Holding faith is an aggressive idea that demands aggressive action. To get the full idea, let's scroll back a verse:

I put this charge before you, Timothy my child, in
keeping with the prophecies once spoken about you, in
order that with such encouragement you may fight the
good fight. To do this you must hold firmly to faith and
a good conscience, which some have rejected and so
have suffered shipwreck in regard to the faith"

—1 TIMOTHY 1:18–19, NET

Holding faith is how we fight the waters. We fight a good fight
through faith and a good conscience. *Holding* here is the Greek
word *echo*, which means "to have (hold) in the hand…in the
sense of wearing…to have (hold) possession of the mind; said of
alarm, agitating emotions, etc."[1]

Faith is like a garment you wear! It is exposed to the elements
and clearly seen.

The Talmud pictures faith as a vehicle to navigate the world's
storms. It keeps us safe and separate from the world. We are not
completely controlled by the waves and changing conditions. Our
ship keeps us from drowning and helps us fight the elements. We
are able to fight a good fight, meaning we progress on our course
and remain stable in rough waters.

I like to bring the modern use of the word *echo* into this scenario: in order to maintain our faith, we must echo what God
says about our circumstances. As we repeat and re-sound the
Word of God in troubled waters, we stay anchored.

KEEP A GOOD CONSCIENCE

The conscience is the platform of our entire point of view and
decision making. *Conscience* is "the inner sense of what is right
or wrong in one's conduct or motives, impelling one toward
right action."[2] When we have a good conscience, we are guided
toward what is right.

Our conscience controls our conduct and our motives.
A good conscience is only conscious of good. God is only

conscious of good, therefore His actions are always good. If you and I have a good conscience, we are good-focused. Titus 1:15 says: "To the *pure all things are pure,* but to those who are defiled and unbelieving nothing is pure; but even their mind and conscience are defiled."

Those who have a pure conscience see all things from a pure perspective. To those who lack a pure conscience, nothing is pure. Their thinking is infected, producing an unbelieving view of life. It is hard to find good in every circumstance when the conscience is defiled. Finding good is an intentional act; without it we interpret everything by emotional default.

To me, the word *defiled* implies that something happened to pollute a good conscience. Something happened to Sarah: she was disappointed. It polluted her point of view and negatively affected key relationships, as the following scripture shows:

> And Sarai said to Abram, "May the wrong done to me
> be on you! I gave my servant to your embrace, and when
> she saw that she had conceived, she looked on me with
> contempt. May the LORD judge between you and me!"
> —GENESIS 16:5, ESV

Sarah made a strong judgment, and her disappointment really began to show. Her conscience was being defiled; it caused her to judge by false weights and balances. Relationships work as long as the scales are balanced. The moment they tip, disappointment arrives to "console" and take charge.

Weight is a standard form of measurement that must apply evenly to all. God is clearly not in agreement with varying standards, as Proverbs 20:10 reveals: "unequal weights and unequal measures are both alike an abomination to the LORD" (ESV).

Standards for weighing and measuring things often matters more to one person than another. This is caused by our cultures, upbringing, and personal convictions. "Little white lies" might be acceptable in some families or cultures, but not in others.

Criminal standards can be more stringent in some areas and more lax elsewhere. When measures are not absolute, a man will believe that it is OK for him to steal from a neighbor's family, but no one had better steal from his.

Why do standards differ and what makes it wrong? Whether they are societal or based upon personal experiences, everyone has standards. Most people get offended when other people disregard their standards. They end up feeling disrespected and even unloved.

My father often made promises that he never fulfilled. Maybe he wanted me to be happy or wanted to show me that he loved me. Yet he never maintained the emotion that prompted the promise long enough to fulfill it. As a result I maintain very high and probably unreasonable standards in this area. If someone promises me that they will do something, my expectation soars.

My unhealthy past has also formed in me unbalanced standards toward commitment. I rarely get excited about people's stated commitments because I have been disappointed in this area. I have learned that people tend to say what other people want to hear, not what needs to be said. This feeds my rationalization of why I shouldn't be excited. My pain raises a standard that only leads me to even greater disappointment.

It would be easy to judge everyone around me for having low standards. I can then reject faith and a good conscience and sink into a depressive state. I have learned to cut this process off. The moment I spot the speck in my brother's eye, I remind myself to deal first with the beam in my own eye (Matt. 7:3).

My beam comes from my standards. I need to keep myself in check and relate to others on their level. Otherwise I will pressure them to make me happy by fulfilling my expectations and dreams.

Sarah had a beam in her eye. She felt unprotected and insecure because Abraham didn't force Hagar to keep up her original duties in serving Sarah. Hagar saw it differently. She had a new status in the family and did not see her former duties as being pertinent anymore.

Everyone's standards were at odds with everyone else's. Instead of being honest and accurate, the weights and balances were false. No one's perception of the situation was exactly right. The missing ingredient was agreement, which depends on all parties being balanced.

So what about Sarah's beam? The key is found in three words from Genesis 16:5: "when she saw." She wasn't the only one seeing things. Everyone saw the situation differently:

- Sarah's perspective was that of a victim. After all, she gave her servant to her husband, who should have kept the servant in check.

- Hagar now saw herself as Sarah's equal. Therefore she felt no need to serve her. After all, she was able to give Abraham the child Sarah could not give him.

- Abraham saw himself as an innocent party. After all, he simply went along with Sarah's plan!

Thankfully there are telltale signs to indicate when we are operating with false weights and balances. The first and most deceptive is excuse making. Disappointed people become very good excuse makers. Even when the reason for their grief is real, the tendency is harmful. It allows them to use the grief to stay "stuck," become prejudiced, or reject God.

What are the signs of an excuse maker? If you haven't accepted responsibility for anything or apologized to someone lately, you might be one. If someone else is always at fault, you are one. If you want others to take responsibility but you prefer not to face the music, excuse making is at work.

Fault finding is not accurately assessing the circumstances. Pointing the finger or throwing someone under the bus is not accurately assessing the circumstances. Another false weight and balance is to do the same thing over and over while expecting a different result.

When Abraham received the promise of a child, his only wife was Sarah. For whatever reason—insecurity, unworthiness, or the thought that someone else was better prepared or more able— she relinquished God's promise and left if for someone else to fulfill. That is a false weight and balance. The promised miracle was not for Abraham and Hagar; it was for Abraham and Sarah.

Contrary to what many people believe, we cannot switch out people like car parts and expect the covenant, the miracle, or the promise to be manifested. No! The promise is made for a specific covenant partnership; altering it in any way can be catastrophic. The switch has proven to be a thorn in the side of Abraham's generations *for generations*.

Things that are born out of season or out of an improper covenant don't die easily. Avoid these situations at all costs! If you have experienced tragic, undesired, and hard-to-understand circumstances and are wondering whether your future is ruined, there is hope. Embrace God's goodness; this is where you need it most! God is bigger and better than the tragedy. He left Job better off than he was before devastation struck. God will be better to you than the pain. If He is to be a good God, He has to deliver you and leave you better off. What He promised is still waiting for you. Receive it with faith, just as though you never took a wrong step.

FIND TRUE NORTH

True north is not open for interpretation. There is only one. Sailors rely on instruments to make sure they are headed the right way. They know they must be correctly guided if they are to safely cross the seas.

In the same manner you and I have to conclude early that we need to be properly guided if we are to survive this life. Putting magnetic north aside for the moment, we need true north and a compass. The Word of God is our true north, and the Holy Spirit is our compass. The Word will never mislead us; neither will the Holy Spirit. They never contradict each other. The Holy Spirit wrote the Bible!

Finding God's true north guarantees that we are "holding the mystery of the faith with a pure conscience" (1 Tim. 3:9). A spirit of confusion convinces many that they can have their own truth. That is a lie. God is truth; Jesus is the Word of truth; and the Holy Spirit is the Spirit of truth. There is no truth without God. Whatever He says is eternally true. Our conscience, when filled with the Word of God and led by the Holy Spirit, will guide us as we navigate the storms of life and complete a successful journey.

KNOW YOUR GRID

On maps, lines of latitude run horizontally and lines of longitude run vertically. Let's begin with latitudes, which are also known as parallels since they are at all points equidistant from one another.

In our spiritual grid lines of latitude are how we relate horizontally, with people. These lines should cause us to become conscious of other people and their needs, even to our own loss:

> But if anyone says to you, "This was offered to idols," do not eat it for the sake of the one who told you, and for conscience' sake; for "the earth is the LORD's, and all its fullness." "Conscience," I say, not your own, but that of the other. For why is my liberty judged by another man's conscience?
>
> —1 CORINTHIANS 10:28–29

Our decisions and conduct must always take other people's consciences into consideration. If we feel a certain activity is OK, but it violates the conscience of a covenant brother or sister, we need to defer to that individual. Although our consciences are clear, we must be sensitive to other people.

Just to be clear: if someone is trying to control or manipulate you, that is another story. Then you must protect *your* conscience. The latitude standard we are discussing is for the sake of keeping a covenant. Someone around you may struggle with alcoholism; even though your glass of wine does not offend your system, abstain for the sake of that person.

A staff member of mine is turned off by a certain slang word. Growing up, he heard the word used in a vulgar way, and it left a bad impression on him. The word is commonly used in a way that is unrelated to his upbringing, but once we found out how it made him feel, the word became dirty to us. Because he is a covenant brother, we changed our ways for his sake.

When we keep the conscience of others in mind, we make room for God to finish His healing process in their lives. As I explained, my standard of commitment stems from a painful part of my past. Some standards are from the Word of God and some need to be healed. Either way, aim high and you will have "a good conscience, so that, when you are slandered, those who revile your good behavior in Christ may be put to shame" (1 Pet. 3:16, ESV).

Now let's talk about longitudes, also known as meridians. These represent our God-consciousness. Everything in our lives should be measured by God's standards. Do you remember the WWJD bracelets from some years ago? The letters represented *What Would Jesus Do?* The bracelets served as constant reminders to see life through God's eyes.

My wife and I work diligently to see all areas of life from an eternal perspective. We zoom out from the circumstances and try to see what it looks like from eternity. Does your life look the same from eternity as it does from within the circumstance? It does not. That's why our habitual question at Citadel

Church is: "What did God say about you before the foundations of the earth?"

When we live with a God consciousness—with His sense of right and wrong, His values, and His worth—we will live differently from the world. We will live and die with honor. I have been moved to live a certain way by Acts 23:1, where Paul declares the secret to his energy and motivation for the gospel: "Looking earnestly at the council, [Paul] said, 'Men and brethren, I have lived in all good conscience before God until this day.'"

Therein is the secret to success! "I have lived in all good conscience before God until this day." God, the creator of all things, has put within our hearts everything that we need to live successful lives. The only way to draw out what He put in us is to never violate a good conscience. Never deny conviction and repentance. Never refuse the promptings of the Lord. Never violate someone else's conscience, whether weak or strong. Scripture tells us that this is extremely important to the Lord, because when "you thus sin against the brethren, and wound their weak conscience, you sin against Christ" (1 Cor. 8:12). God doesn't see violating someone's conscience as a sin against them; it is a sin against His Son.

The patriarchs, apostles, and disciples endured many things, but never stopped believing in God. They counted it an honor to withstand persecution and hardship for His standard. As Peter wrote: "This is commendable, if *because of conscience toward God* one endures grief, suffering wrongfully" (1 Pet. 2:19).

Even when persecuted, we must not lower our standard and violate our God consciousness. Being persecuted is commendable when we keep our standard high. We are to win others to Christ, but not by acquiescing to worldly ideals. Imposing our standards on them is not God's way, either. Neither is rejecting them. But we must not reject His truth for their sakes. That would be taking our latitudinal standards too far.

Hold your longitudes firm, and God will commend your faith in His goodness.

FIND A SAFE HARBOR

Our third and final standard for navigating the storms of life is to make sure that we have a safe harbor. When life is overwhelming, Christ is your safe harbor. Maybe you have violated your conscience and you feel that you have drifted too far from shore. It might seem as if your compass and your grid have gone missing. But whatever the challenge or failure Christ is able to rescue you!

Jesus is the way, the truth, and the life (John 14:6). He is in the lighthouse, constantly searching for those who need His help. As you approach the harbor, you can easily get His attention. Just wave and ask for His help. You might be hopelessly adrift, hanging onto a small slab of wood to stay afloat. All He needs is for you to believe He can help, and He will immediately show up.

When I was young, I hit a very tough place in life and became desperate. Everything I did failed. I didn't believe in God; I actually hated Him and was ready to fight at the mention of Jesus's name. One day when I'd had enough, I considered suicide, but I didn't know what would happen after death. "Things can't get worse," I thought. "I'll try anything."

Eventually I knelt down by my bed and prayed: "God if You are real, show me!" Suddenly a picture of Jesus from my grandmother's house flashed in my mind. I did not immediately accept Jesus as the answer, but I did start believing in God that day. Not long after that I was introduced to Jesus as my Lord and Savior. I found my safe harbor!

CLEANSED!

Hebrews 9:14 asks: "How much more shall the blood of Christ, who through the eternal Spirit offered Himself without spot to God, cleanse your conscience from dead works to serve the living God?"

God didn't walk into my room as I knelt by my bed. He did start the process of cleaning my conscience with the blood of Jesus. That is what makes the harbor safe—the blood of Jesus! It not only washes away our sins, but it also cleanses the human conscience of any dead, nonproductive, harmful deeds.

Paul the apostle, once known as Saul, spoke more about a pure conscience than anyone else in the Bible. Why? Could it be that the grateful always talk about what they are grateful for? Paul had to be grateful to have all the murders he performed washed from his conscience. You cannot kill all those people, including women and children, without it affecting your conscience. (I believe this will help soldiers coming home from war: an encounter with the blood of Jesus will cleanse your conscience from the things you have seen and partaken of.) Once the blood of Jesus cleansed Paul, the faces of his victims were erased from his conscience.

So many people believe they are too far gone for saving. That is not God speaking; it is the voice of a bad conscience. God is good conscious. He is not mad at you. His response to your bad deeds and thoughts was Jesus. Jesus came *because* God is not mad at you. He died so you can stop being mad at yourself, other people, and God.

When your conscience is clean, the bad and the mad are washed away. The only thing you are left with is a good conscience. Then you will start focusing on the good in others. And as you receive the blood of Jesus, you will experience true forgiveness and repentance.

It is important to mention that repentance is different from forgiveness. A personal anecdote illustrates my point. It started when a minister told me that he was mad at God. It was the third time that week that I heard of someone being mad at God. I went home puzzled and bothered, really.

I asked my wife, "How could anyone be mad at God?"

She responded, "You used to be mad at God!"

"No way!" I protested.

She just looked at me and smiled. Then the Holy Spirt reminded me of a tantrum I'd had in the past. The video played in my head, and I saw myself saying, "God, I am so mad at You!"

I couldn't help but laugh out loud. I had totally forgotten that I used to be mad at God a lot. I wondered, "How could I forget all the rants I gave God?"

Suddenly the thought came: "It's the goodness of God that leads to repentance" (Rom. 2:4). I leapt up, realizing that I had forgotten about being mad at God because I stopped seeing God as a bad God. Once I recognized His goodness, my conscience was cleansed of even the memory of my former anger.

Imagine that you buy a new car. Then every day for a year you listen to the car radio. The sound is good, but it is not the sound you really want. Suddenly you spot a tiny button that you never noticed before. It says, "Good."

You think to yourself, "What does *that* do?" So you push the button. Bam! Everything changes. The music no longer sounds as if it's in a can. Now it sounds as though the band were in the car with you. You are so happy to have found a button that changes everything! From that point on each time you turn on the stereo, you hit the "Good" button, without even thinking. You don't even remember what it sounded like before you found the button, and you don't ever want to go back. You have repented from mediocre sound. Now you expect the best sound all the time.

That's repentance! It's forgetting the bad parts that happened. Forgiveness is letting it go, but repentance is when it is gone and no longer an issue. The blood of Jesus causes us to repent. It causes us to forget the bad and see only the good.

You have been given divine instruments of navigation. You are destined for true north.

Part Two

I Believe

Chapter 9

I CAN CHANGE IT

The power of change is a simple but potent revelation: *I can!* As with any revelation, this one can only be experienced and received by faith, which is the currency of heaven. The power to change anything—the power to overcome disappointment and learn the art of joy—must include faith.

Without faith, King David would have fainted at the sight of pursuing enemies (Ps. 27:13). Faith was and is the game changer. Jesus's disciples knew David's testimony but still had much to learn about faith. Jesus gave them a primer during a fierce storm:

> When he [Jesus] was entered into a ship, his disciples followed him. And, behold, there arose a great tempest in the sea, insomuch that the ship was covered with the waves: but he was asleep. And his disciples came to him, and awoke him, saying, Lord, save us: we perish.
> —Matthew 8:23–25, kjv

It is interesting that we allow courage to flee even when Jesus is in our boat. The disciples' reaction is common. It is a sign of those who have lost heart. The Bible commands us to keep our hearts, much the way we would say, "Be courageous." Courage is a form of faith that looks every challenge in the eye and *knows* that it is subject to change.

When things are moving in multiple directions and even coming apart, we need to keep from hardening our hearts. The moment our hearts fail from alarming circumstances, we must make a choice. We will either keep our hearts soft and embrace the possibility of good coming from the situation, or we will give ourselves to faithlessness, hopelessness, and desperation, fully trusting the worst.

The first choice is much better! Believing for something good to happen releases God's creative ability in and through us. One of the great benefits of having Jesus in your boat is the ability to meet with Him directly whenever your faith is challenged. Even if you think He's sleeping while you are drowning, He's in command. Jesus slept during the disciples' storm on purpose. It was not because He did not love them or want to help them. He knew they possessed the faith to change their circumstances—and they needed to know it too.

Is that what Jesus is doing with you? Is He pointing out the fact that you have what it takes to bring the change you need? Is it possible that you are already powerful enough to handle the situation, but you are not yet convinced?

When Sarah complained to Abraham about the tangled-up circumstance involving the now pregnant Hagar, his response was clean and precise: "Behold, your servant is in your power; do to her as you please" (Gen. 16:6, ESV).

What a powerful truth: we should never complain about anything we are unwilling to do something about. Only people who feel powerless complain. Empowered people act. They don't waste their time complaining; they use their time making things happen.

To overcome complaining, the first step is recognizing that *everything* is subject to change. Defeat and disappointment are not static states, but if something is going to change, you have to change it using the power you have already received.

Abraham gently and kindly encouraged Sarah to take charge by making a decision. "Your servant is in your power," he said, reminding her that Hagar was still a servant. In other words, "Sarah, she is still under your command. Do what you would normally do."

Abraham was not suggesting an unseemly action. He simply expected Sarah to use her power to choose. Hagar was still subject to Sarah's command, just as your circumstances are subject to yours. You already possess the power to bring about the desired changes. Just decide!

This is not my idea; it is God's. As Paul wrote: "I can do all things through Christ who strengthens me" (Phil. 4:13). Paul showed us how to tap into God's strength. Notice it is attached to our "I can." Before we can use His strength, we must recognize our ability to bring change.

God needs your "I can"! Don't be shy about saying, "I can do anything that God can do through me!"

Do you remember the story I shared about moving from San Diego to Seattle? God led Nathalie and me to take over a faltering church in an economically depressed area. I was confident that my training in coaching would help lift the people out of their discouragement and lack. Instead, I discovered that their "I can't!" drowned out my "You can!"

Philippians 4:13 can make a congregation shout for joy, but until we process our perception of past experiences and discover our "I can," *we can't.* What is in our hearts determines how we deal with challenges, blessings, and responsibilities. Strength is not the real issue: Jesus's strength is always available to us. The challenge is whether we have put our "I can'ts" to rest so that we can use the strength He has given us.

So what is your immediate responsibility? It is to realize that your decisions determine how things turn out. If you keep making today's decisions on the basis of previous ones, you will keep getting the old results. If divorce is in your rearview mirror and your ex is a nightmare, start making decisions that force you to raise your standard. Look at the situation from a new perspective. Reject knee-jerk reactions that cause you to complain and react in negative ways.

That was Abraham's advice to Sarah: "Stop living in the past and take charge of your now." In other words, reconcile yourself with the fact that you made a poor decision that is currently affecting your life. To change the story and heal the pain, another decision must be made. Don't become paralyzed, fearing yet another mistake. Your past mistakes cannot erase today's good choices.

Taking responsibility for past failures is not something most people want to do. In the short term it is easier to fix the blame elsewhere. The benefit of taking responsibility is that having learned something from your last mistake, you will be postured to move ahead.

If you don't take responsibility today, you will have to learn the lesson someday, somehow. Taking responsibility is empowering. Admit your past failures and move on.

NO FEAR, JUST FAITH...AND WORDS

We have seen that excuse making is a form of weakness. Excuses are fear based and designed to absolve us from responsibility. They are not reasons. They tend to be *unreasonable.* If a relationship breaks apart, there is usually some fault on both sides. It is unreasonable to lay all the blame on one party. Even if there are valid reasons for what happened, there is no place for excuses.

Excuse makers neutralize their ability to learn and their power to change the very situations they want to see transformed. The energy that goes into creating the excuse and blaming someone else would be more profitably used to generate a decision that can turn the situation around.

Sarah needed a turnaround in her relationships. Scripture says she treated Hagar harshly (Gen. 16:6). After some research into rabbinical teaching, I found that Sarah treated Hagar just as she did when Hagar first came to serve her. Hagar thought it harsh to be put in her proper place.

Whenever you attempt to put back in order things that have gone off track, it will likely be seen as a harsh activity. Change will always be resisted; but you cannot restore order without change. Don't lose heart when change is resisted and labeled *harsh*. Yes, it will seem as though a storm has broken out in your home, office, or ministry. Just anchor yourself until the storm passes.

Paul suffered many things but always anchored himself in His relationship with God. He believed it was the key to having strength to achieve anything and everything. Paul lived from this belief: "If God can do it, He can do it through me."

Paul had an anchor. You have one too, but you have to use it. An anchor must be cast into the water. It is of no use until it is. It's not enough to have an "I can" in your heart. You must cast it forth with your mouth.

Paul declared in Philippians, "I can do all things." In Acts he declared a good ending while sailing on a seemingly doomed ship. When everyone despaired of life, Paul said, "Sirs, be of good cheer: for I believe God, that it shall be even as it was told me" (Acts 27:25, KJV). Paul did not lose his "I can" in the storm. He continued speaking it out and stood firm.

The storm was a serious one. Like a huge hurricane, it would have prevented Paul and the crew from seeing clearly. The boat was beaten by the waves, and the crew threw cargo overboard. Everyone but Paul thought this was the end. But when Paul stood up, he spoke from faith. He said, "I *believe* God, that it shall be even as it was told me."

Believers speak what they believe. If you truly believe, you cannot help but say what you believe. Jesus spoke to a tree, and the tree obeyed (Matt. 21:19). The Father spoke to light and it also obeyed (Gen. 1:3). Jesus said that whatever we say in prayer we shall receive, even when we tell mountains to move (Mark 11:22–24).

Jesus was specific. He did not say that whatever we thought, wished, hoped, and believed would come to pass. Of course we must do all those things. But it is our commanding and authoritative speech in prayer that brings results. We don't command God; we agree with Him, worship Him, and love Him in prayer. Then we speak to things that must change. We speak to trees, mountains, voids, dead places and things—whatever needs to be aligned with God's will.

Our speaking is not for show or fun. We have divine authority to speak His instruction to people, places, and things. God gave us His spirit of faith. It will keep our hearts light. When problems come, we refuse to hand over our hearts to fear. We give our hearts to God by stating what we believe. What we believe has our hearts.

Jesus encouraged us to keep our hearts from trouble by believing in God and in Christ (John 14:1). This is faith! We either believe in them or we believe in trouble. When we believe in God, we trust His authority more than we trust our circumstances. This faith keeps us from fainting. Remember: hope is expectation and faith is hope's foundation. Faith is more than a feeling. It is a force!

Galatians 5:6 says that faith works through love. The Greek word translated "works" in this verse is *energeo*. It means "to be active, efficient…[to] do, (be) effectual (fervent), be mighty in, shew forth self, work (effectually in)."[1] Faith is activated and made effective through love. *Energeo* is the root of our English word *energy*. So faith gets its energy from love. Love and faith then make us powerful enough to bring about the proper and desired change.

In James 5 this same word is used to describe Elijah's prayer for rain. Effective and fervent prayers force much to happen. Energetic prayers are not necessarily loud or physically and emotionally exuberant. But they must possess faith energized through love in order to be effective.

Notice that "Elijah was a man with a nature like ours, and he prayed fervently that it might not rain, and for three years and six months it did not rain on the earth" (James 5:17, ESV). Just because you and I are natural human beings doesn't mean that we cannot move things supernaturally. We *can*, through faith-filled prayers energized by love.

First Corinthians 13:7–8 says that love believes and never fails. That is the basis of real faith. Faith that never fails is energized by love.

STOCKPILE FAITH (AND PATIENCE)

In modern society we stockpile things we know we will need in the future. For Y2K we stockpiled beans, toilet paper, and water. Many of us work hard every day to stockpile money. We stock-pile business cards in hopes of networking with the right people at the right time. We stockpile baseball cards as a hobby. We stockpile stuff!

Years ago I was prompted to stockpile faith instead of what-ever else I was working so hard to put aside for a rainy day. It's not that we shouldn't have savings accounts or make wise invest-ments. I just needed to stop trusting plans, people, places, and things, I needed to start trusting God.

I am a strategist and a planner; I like to see what's ahead and how to deal with it. Because of my nature I can easily miss the mark by trusting in my strategies. This is where my biggest frus-trations, regrets, and disappointments have come from.

The Bible makes it clear that a man is right in his own eyes, but the Lord directs his steps (Prov. 21:2). As Moses told the Israelites, we are not to follow our ideas, but God's:

> You shall not do according to all that we are doing here today, everyone doing whatever is right in his own eyes, for you have not as yet come to the rest and to the inheritance that the LORD your God is giving you. But when you go over the Jordan and live in the land that the LORD your God is giving you to inherit, and when he gives you rest from all your enemies around, so that you live in safety, then to the place that the LORD your God will choose, to make his name dwell there, there you shall bring all that I command you: your burnt offerings and your sacrifices, your tithes and the contribution that you present, and all your finest vow offerings that you vow to the LORD.
> —DEUTERONOMY 12:8–11, ESV

The full context of this passage is amazing. God wanted His people to understand that they were not to act like heathens who trust in things. They had to put their trust in Him. This was their ticket into the rest and possession of the Promised Land.

God instituted a system of trusting Him through tithes and offerings. Through giving we show that we trust in Him more than in plans, people, places, and things. Obedience in tithes and offerings is a form of stockpiling faith for the future.

Malachi presented the concept this way:

> Bring the full tithe into the storehouse, that there may be food in my house. And thereby put me to the test, says the LORD of hosts, if I will not open the windows of heaven for you and pour down for you a blessing until there is no more need. I will rebuke the devourer for you, so that it will not destroy the fruits of your soil, and your vine in the field shall not fail to bear, says the LORD

of hosts. Then all nations will call you blessed, for you
will be a land of delight, says the LORD of hosts.

                                        —MALACHI 3:10–12, ESV

The New Testament confirms this life of stockpiling faith
through obedience and giving. The rich young ruler, the widow
and her mite, Paul's letters to the Corinthians and Philippians
(e.g., 2 Cor. 9; Phil. 4)—these demonstrate the faith and fruit
of giving.

It is absolutely necessary for us to put our faith in God and
nothing else if we are going to have the power to change problems and remove limitations. Jesus told the disciples as much
when they said their faith was lacking:

> The apostles said to the Lord, *"Increase* our faith!" And
> the Lord said, "If you had faith like a grain of mustard
> seed, you could say to this mulberry tree, 'Be uprooted
> and planted in the sea,' and it would obey you."
>
>   —LUKE 17: 5–6, ESV

Increase in the Greek means "to place additionally, i.e. lay
beside, annex."[2] Jesus replied that if we have faith like a seed
(meaning, if we would liken our faith to a seed) then we would
discover how to increase it. How? By planting it!

The way we plant our faith seed is to speak our desire out loud.
That means saying what we expect to happen. God said, "Light
be!" and it was (Gen. 1:3). He created us with the same ability to
speak with authority. Now we say what we desire and it is. God
made us speaking spirits according to the Hebrew text, which
has been translated in English as "living soul" (Gen. 2:7, ASV).
We were created to speak what we believe. As we plant it, our
belief increases.

Jesus simply told His disciples to talk like God. He encouraged
them saying, "You could say to this mulberry tree, 'Be uprooted
and planted in the sea,' and it would obey you" (Luke 17:6, ESV).

In other words, speak as though your request was already done—and it will be done!

We are not supposed to speak what we *wish* would happen, but what we *expect* to happen. God didn't rebuke the darkness, or say, "I wish it weren't so dark." He spoke what He wanted: light to replace darkness. Jesus did the same thing when He told the lame man to walk and the man was healed (John 5).

If there is a mountain in the way, tell it to move. If something is missing, tell it to come. Use your words to increase your faith until your faith overtakes your want. That is the key—more faith than want. Psalm 23:1 says: "The LORD is my shepherd; I *shall not* want." When the Lord is your shepherd, all your wants are taken care of. There is no want when you believe that.

The Bible says Abraham walked before God (Gen. 17:1; 24:40, KJV). In other words, Abraham trusted God for all of his sustenance. The more we trust God, the more *want* will leave our lives.

I told you about how my kids acted whenever I promised to take them to Disneyland. All they needed to know was that Daddy promised. They never worried that I might change my mind or ask them to pay up. They just asked, "Is it time yet?"

The writer of Hebrews encouraged Jewish believers to have the same confident faith:

> We desire each one of you to show the same earnestness to have the full assurance of hope until the end, so that you may not be sluggish, but imitators of those who through faith and patience inherit the promises.
>
> —HEBREWS 6:11–12, ESV

It is critical to maintaining faith, hope, and love. It holds them together and makes it possible to endure the hardships, distractions, and disappointments that must be endured to realize the prize.

Through faith and patience we inherit the promise. Isn't that funny! An inheritance is a gift, not a reward. We must keep the same faith from beginning to end if we are to receive our inheritance. But the hardest part can be to "have the full assurance of hope until the end." We must strive to maintain the same level of passion, faith, and expectation until the inheritance is received.

My number one frustration as an entrepreneur and church planter is that people get excited about a vision but don't know how to keep the intensity going till the end. Excitement has stages. The first stage is passive, meaning that we get excited about what's possible, but we believe based upon an external influence. The next stage of excitement is aggressiveness and proactivity.

Excitement must be maintained through internal processes, with daily adjustments to our levels of faith and patience. Think of faith and patience as workers. Notice what Scripture says: "Let patience have her perfect work, that ye may be perfect and entire, wanting nothing" (James 1:4, KJV).

The job of patience is to set you free from want as you become more and more perfected and complete. Your words will always reveal how your patience is working. From your mouth your heart speaks. So let patience perfect and complete you. Patience will not only make you powerful, but you will become a powerhouse, a source of energy for others. Jesus was both:

> He saith unto them, Why are ye fearful, O ye of little faith? Then he arose, and rebuked the winds and the sea; and there was a great calm. But the men marvelled, saying, What manner of man is this, that even the winds and the sea obey him!
> —MATTHEW 8:26–27, KJV

Jesus was such a powerhouse that His disciples were continually amazed by His authority. Even after spending many days and hours with Him, they had to ask: "What manner of man is this?"

God's intention in sending Jesus was not completed when Jesus delivered and saved us. He is also our big brother whose job is to teach and instruct His siblings how to work in the Father's dream and do the Father's business. To fulfill His purpose, it is not enough for Jesus to be powerful; He must also make us powerful.

Jesus was so deeply at rest in the boat that the winds and the waves didn't wake Him. It seems He was confident that the wind and waves *couldn't* awaken Him. Jesus wasn't at all concerned for His life.

The same cannot be said for His disciples. Their faith dwindled with every crashing wave. They wondered why Jesus did nothing about the storm. We often do the same thing. We think God should save us, so we pray. Has it occurred to us that Jesus expected His disciples to handle the storm so He could get some sleep?

Apparently it had not occurred to the disciples. They woke Jesus and asked Him if He cared whether or not they perished (Mark 4:38). Their words revealed that their faith and patience were challenged. So Jesus asked, "Why are ye fearful, O ye of little faith?" (Matt. 8:26, KJV).

Jesus recognized that fear was taking over and faith was getting small. Much of the disciples' faith, hope, and love were snatched by the wind and waves. Their little faith woke Jesus, but their increasing fear questioned His love and care. They possessed both: a little faith and a little fear.

That was the wrong mixture! The goal is to be fully possessed of faith, allowing no room for fear. Just as God replaced darkness with light in the beginning, we should replace fear with faith. To do this, we must understand that faith is not a fixed amount, but it's like a seed—not the size of a seed, but faithful and patient like a seed that lasts a long time and grows through the storm.

Seeds grow bigger than what they were in the beginning. To reach their full potential, seeds need soil. Likewise, faith needs time. If we pick it too early, the full potential is lost. The product is not ripe or mature. It lacks its full complement of nutrients and is short on flavor.

Jesus let His disciples know that their faith was not so much small, but immature. They needed more practice to grow it.

What did the disciples expect Jesus to do? I doubt they had a specific expectation other than wanting Jesus to end their crisis and save them. We often approach God the same way—with no expectation. It's not enough to be saved. We should always expect victory. Jesus showed His disciples how trials should be handled. He stood in the boat as waves slammed it and wind blew sea mist in His face and said, "Peace, be still!" (Mark 4:39), which is "Shhhhh…be quiet!"

That's right! Your circumstances are talking to you. The waves and the winds are talking to you. The storm talked to the disciples and convinced them that they were in trouble. So they surrendered their faith to the circumstances.

The moment Jesus spoke to the winds and told them what He wanted them to do, the winds obeyed. Peace replaced the chaos, just as Jesus commanded. He knew the disciples had the same spirit of faith He did. He knew they could have quieted the winds themselves. That is why He kept sleeping!

Maybe God is not moving as quickly as you'd like to save you from your problems because He knows that you possess the faith and patience to change them. Peter, James, John, Matthew—any one of the disciples could have stood at the edge of the boat and told the storm to shut up and be quiet, and the winds would have obeyed him.

We spend too much time trying to escape our storms. Not Jesus! He understood that the storm was not designed to kill Him, but to reveal Him. No wonder the disciples asked, "What kind of man is this that even the winds and the sea obey him?"

The storm revealed a side of Jesus they had never seen. Your storm is revealing in you something no one has ever seen before. The powerhouse in you is being awakened. Don't stop short on your faith and forfeit this opportunity to reveal your full potential. Let patience join you in the process. Let the storm reveal what kind of person you are.

You have the power to change everything that doesn't belong in your life. Know that *you can*, then tell the storm, "Peace, be still!"

Chapter 10

IT'S ABOUT TIME

The Bible records the conception and birth of Adam and Eve's first son, Cain. It also mentions the birth of another boy named Abel. (See Genesis 4:1–2.) Both Cain and Abel were hard workers. Cain worked the ground and Abel was a shepherd. A particular quote gets my attention: "In the *process of time* it came to pass that Cain brought an offering of the fruit of the ground to the LORD" (Gen. 4:3).

What is *the process of time*? In Hebrew it would be *yom qets*, which, according to Strong's concordance, means "day of end, at the end of time, end of space." This was not a usual, normal day. This was the day to bring the offering. It was a specific day that ended one time period and started another.

When one time ends, another starts. When the last hour leaves, a new one begins. This was obviously a day that the Lord had set to end something and start something new. We refer to this kind of time as *kairos*, a supreme moment describing a specific time.

Cain brought his offering to the "Day of the End" or "Day of New Space" festival, which had to have been planned ahead by God. Cain and Abel had to be informed of the timing and of how to prepare a pleasing offering for God. But something went wrong for Cain. Neither he nor his offering was respected by God. However, Abel and his offering were pleasing to Him.

It is worth noting that although God did not respect Cain and his offering, He did not reject Cain. God is so good that He can separate His feelings for us from His feelings regarding the things we do.

God might not like your lifestyle, but that doesn't mean He loves you less. Yet offense entered Cain's heart when God responded negatively to his offering but positively to his brother's. Cain's own feelings of rejection and comparison angered him. Deep disappointment led to great bitterness in Cain's soul.

God addressed Cain's condition:

> He [the LORD] did not respect Cain and his offering. And Cain was very angry, and his countenance fell. So the LORD said to Cain, "*Why are you angry?* And *why has your countenance fallen?*"
>
> —GENESIS 4:5–6

When God wants you to see yourself, He often will ask you a question rather than tell you what is wrong. His intent is to take you to your next level. On the way there, however, you will have the opportunity to take offense. God takes advantage of these opportunities to train you by asking probing questions about why you feel the way you do. He does not ask to antagonize you, but to prepare you for advancement.

Rabbinical teaching tells us that in objecting to Cain's offering, God wanted to teach him the power of repentance. He wanted Cain to change his mind about the circumstance and grow from the experience.

Moving to the next level is not possible unless you repent (by changing your mind) regarding the last level. Maybe you are still angry about something that you should have seen differently. If you think that anger will leave at the next level, you will be surprised by this fact: the thing you are angry about is preventing your next level.

That was God's message to Cain. He wanted Cain to advance, so He asked him two questions: "*Why* are you angry? And *why* has your countenance fallen?"

These were heart questions that dealt with Cain's character. When He said, "What's up with your face?" that meant, "I can tell something is mixed up on the inside." Cain's outward expression reflected an internal issue. So God allowed the perfect circumstances to expose it.

Attitude shows up at key times. It may be that God wanted Cain's hidden attitudes revealed so that He could change his mind about them. Bad attitudes cannot be rewarded. People with attitude issues should never be exalted while the attitude continues. The attitude should be worked out before they are given passage to the next level.

WATCH YOUR DOORS

Doors represent opportunity. Where doors are discussed, there is usually talk about timing. God sets doors of opportunity at the right times in our lives. People generally miss these doors not because they lack talent or ability, but because they are distracted.

Genesis 4:7 holds the secrets to promotion: "If you do well, will you not be accepted? And if you do not do well, sin is crouching at the door" (ESV). It's simple: do good things and you will be elevated and exalted. This is the key to your next level. This assumes that you know what is right, which Cain did. Yet in preparing his offering, he did not choose the right way. He chose the lesser way and did what was unpleasing to God.

God is good and desires His children to be motivated by good. This is the key to reaching the elevation you desire and not finding sin crouched at your door. Let me properly translate "do well" to "be good." Being good exalts you; it is about more than

doing good things. It is about being good through and through
to your core so your conduct will follow and you will be elevated.

Do you want to go higher in your life, marriage, ministry, and
business? Be good! The contrast with the alternative is amazing:
be elevated or be hunted down by sin. Sin lies in wait for those
who are up to no good. It will sabotage any chance you have for
advancement and will present its own dark opportunities.

Doors are about timing and access. As access points they
close off one space and open another. When a giant opportunity
comes, we say that we have an open door. God sets doors as ele-
vators to take us up, not at a random time but on a certain day
ordained for next-level movement.

There is no allowance to skip levels or to occupy an old one
and a new one at the same time. We must have a *yom qets*. That
is when we can go through the door and achieve our dreams.

All of this assumes the avoidance of the sin trap. This is a door
none of us can afford to open. Sin, offense, and disappointment
lurk at the door to control us, our emotions, our decisions, and
our lives. It wants to be our lord and ruler. If we are looking for
good, we won't choose sin; we will choose the promise. This is
the door of God's presence, voice, and goodness.

Every door of opportunity is surrounded by distractions—lots
of them. They include voices speaking in other languages. You
hear the ones that speak *your* language. The door of sin favors
certain words and questions. Its voice asks: "Why?" and "Why
did You let this happen? Why didn't You stop me? Why should
I trust You?"

Many people live with these questions daily. I know I lived
with the voice of regret often. We should not enter every door,
but we should choose the door of God's presence, listening for
the sounds of His goodness and for insight into His timing.

The voice at this door poses healthier questions: "How? How
should I proceed? How should I think or feel? How should I
position myself? How should my attitude look as I wait?" This

is the voice of wisdom giving instructions for the next season. It is where Sarah heard that she would give birth one year from right now (Gen. 18:10). She heard it while listening at the door of God's presence. Rest assured that such a confirmation will never be found while listening at the door of offense.

A lame man begged for alms at a gate called Beautiful (Acts 3). *Beautiful* means: "belonging to the right time or season."[1] This is an appointed time, a *kairos* time. It is important that we camp out at our appointed time in faith. We do that by fully believing that something good is coming and by watching expectantly for it to be fulfilled. We might not know when or how, but we can be sure that it will happen. The vision will not lie, because it is for an appointed time (Hab. 2:3).

Paul the apostle shed light on the subject of doors of opportunity by mentioning one that he entered: "For a *great* and *effective* door has opened to me, and there are *many adversaries*" (1 Cor. 16:9). Paul was talking about a door where sin lurked. The door was not a door of sin, but adversaries were there to prevent him from entering a divinely appointed opportunity.

Paul saw "a great and effective door." It was a huge door, or *megas*,[2] door in the Greek. This is a familiar word. Stores have mega sales. Mega-club membership stores sell bottled water in mega-size packaging. Paul was looking at a door of *mega* opportunity.

Working with people for as many years as I have, I have seen them respond to mega doors in surprisingly "mini" ways. Maybe an unsaved husband gets saved after putting his wife through twenty years of hell and unending prayer. Instead of being thrilled, the wife feels frustrated, as though the spouse got off too easy for giving her such a hard time. It sounds almost unbelievable, but it happens. It is offense in action.

Other people say they want more of God but get offended when He starts moving in their lives. In answer to their prayers He opens the next level. Instead of being thankful, they dislike new things. Life looks different from a higher elevation, and they are not so sure they like it. So they harbor disappointment.

We have worked for years with volunteer staff members who were being prepared for paid positions. Just as they approach the threshold of that door, they suddenly become careless or lazy. Sometimes they get restless and leave to do something else—*just before the promotion comes.* There is a noticeable pattern of unwitting self-sabotage when the prayed-for opportunity finally arrives.

Paul uses another word to describe the door God opened for him. It was not only *megas,* but also *energes.* It is translated "effective," which means "active"[3] as a form of power or a level of energy would be. To embrace the open door, we must keep putting energy toward it, actively pursuing with tenacity and intensity.

To push past the adversaries that are trying to prevent us, we must approach these doors with both a mega mind-set and a mega energy level. Sin is at the door, whether your heart is right or wrong. It will find a hook in you if your heart is bad. If your heart is good, there is no hook to find. Sin might talk to you, but it will not distract you from your goal.

Paul mentions adversaries at the door. God disclosed sin waiting at the door for Cain. These are one and the same. Sin is usually something that has already been partaken of. James says that we are drawn away by the sin in our hearts (James 1:14–15). Often we experience temptations in cyclical fashion. Each year the same temptation comes around again. Perhaps depression comes at the same time, year after year. Or certain illnesses become cyclical.

The enemy's attacks are systematic and strategic. He works hard to harm you through trials and temptations. He hopes that a little hook will remain in you even after you are sure you worked through the issue itself. His goal is that you would think you are all healed up, only to find that every circumstance that reminds you of what happened in the past causes you to respond anew.

Familiar Doors and Covenant

I told you about the rottweiler that attacked my wife when she was very young. To this day Nathalie is very conscious of large dogs. I understand the emotional marker such an event can leave behind. Having never been bitten by a dog, my level of caution around them is lower than Nathalie's is. Such reminders of past events tend to revisit us when future doors open. They crouch there hoping to find some remnant of a hook through which they can make fresh inroads.

Our God is a God of covenant. He has spoken something about each of us from before the foundations of the world. He is actively working to open doors that will get us into the right place at the right time with the right people.

The enemy is not OK with that. He's not just afraid of your making it into your open door; he is also concerned about how many people's lives you will touch on the other side of it. Covenant relationships will be involved in pursuing, reaching, and inhabiting your new space. That is what the story of Cain's and Abel's offerings is really about. More than a lesson about offerings, it is the story of a covenant relationship between brothers who were going to the next level together. To go higher, they had to become each other's keeper. Cain needed Abel and Abel needed Cain. They needed each other's gifts and abilities to survive.

They also needed to work together before they brought their offerings to the Lord. Both offerings should have included a blood sacrifice as Abel's did. Cain needed to trade some of his produce for a lamb to offer the Lord. The offering structure had been already set, and Cain knew it. But he did not want to be kept by his brother; nor did he want to keep Abel. So he stepped out from the covenant.

When a covenant is broken, a door will inevitably be missed and timing will be thrown off. The adversary wants to steal your time, kill your future, and destroy all of your covenants along the way. This adversary is not your "normal enemy," but one that thinks he has the perfect trap for you.

Satan is crafty. When we approach open doors, we come ready to fight, but not ready to resist what's familiar. The spirit of familiarity was Cain's downfall. This destructive force fights viciously against covenant relationships by creating offense. Jesus warned: "Woe to the world because of offenses! For offenses must come, but woe to that man by whom the offense comes!" (Matt. 18:7).

The world would be amazing if offense were not possible. But because of the Fall and because everything in the world is based upon agreement and covenant, offense is possible. As usual, studying the topic from the original text rather than later translations provides a fuller understanding. The word translated "offenses" is *skandalon,* from which we get our English word, *scandal.* It means "the movable stick or trigger of a trap, a trap stick a trap, snare, any impediment placed in the way and causing one to stumble or fall, (a stumbling block, occasion of stumbling)."[4]

Skandalon, the sin at the door in Genesis 4, is the same trap as the adversaries mentioned in 1 Corinthians 16:9. It's an offense! The enemy uses familiarity to distract us away from newly opened doors and back into old habits, agreements, or covenant relationships. If we are not alert, we can easily sacrifice the new for the old.

Like me, you probably know people who can't seem to drop their old patterns. Each time they go after something new, the old voice woos them back again. Going backward is easier than going forward because visiting familiar places is easier than visiting unknown ones. Never will something new hold you back from your open door; always it will be something old.

Anytime we are offended, we know a trap was set to distract us from a mega opportunity involving a covenant relationship. Every one of us has had this experience. According to the definition of *skandalon,* it's a trigger of a trap set by a third party (someone outside the covenant relationship under attack). The adversary is after covenant relationships, and will not reveal himself as he sets traps between husbands and wives, siblings, business partners, neighbors, pastors and church members, parents and children.

Here's an example of how the trap works: you spot a friend at the supermarket and walk up and say, "Hello!" Your friend is caught off guard and seems aloof. You exchange a few words and part ways. As you walk away, you feel uneasy about the relationship and begin to interpret the uneasy feeling. You think, "She doesn't like me."

You even imagine hearing your friend's thoughts: "I don't like her. Her hair is weird. She gets on my nerves."

Without realizing it, you are fashioning an offense in your heart toward your friend. Completely convinced that she dislikes you, you put your guard up when you see her the following week. Strangely enough she seems happy to see you this time but notices that your response is different.

You cut the conversation short. Now *she* feels rejected and walks away thinking, "What's wrong with her? Maybe I did something wrong. Well, I didn't like her anyway!"

A few days later you run into each other again. This time both of you are too busy to talk. "Hi, sorry, I can't talk. I'm in a big hurry!" she says.

"Yes, same here. Bye!" you chime in.

The relationship has begun to unravel. You both allow years to go by without talking. Then you spot each other at a gathering. You end up talking, and she tells you what happened that first time at the store. She explains that she had just been to the doctor, who gave her an alarming test result. She was a little bit out of it when you spotted her, but by the second chance meeting the doctor assured her that her condition was not life-threatening. She confides in you, saying that she has missed the relationship you once shared and could have used your friendship over the past three years.

A funny look from a friend was interpreted as rejection. The trap was sprung. The offense was locked in. The enemy used scandals from the past to interrupt opportunities for the future. It was never just between two friends, either. The third party—the adversary—was behind it all.

As a young minister I was zealous to do God's work. My methods were unconventional, not because I was rebellious, but because I didn't know any different. My gift made room for me and brought me before mature leaders. Because my ministry style was unrefined, I found myself called into many meetings to discuss it. After awhile I felt more attacked than helped. My disappointment deepened, and my guard went up to the point that whenever I was called to minister for someone new, I raised a wall of pride and arrogance. I told myself I didn't need them; they needed me.

This air was evident around me. The result was not good. I ended up sabotaging God-given relationships. I later regretted acting in such a way and realized that God's mega opportunities usually involve people! Just as Cain would never have a pleasing offering without Abel's help, I could not enter my next level without covenant relationships. They had something I needed, and I had something they needed.

When I realized the damage I had done to these relationships, I took Paul's advice to heart: I sought to forget the things that were behind me, and press on to the higher level of my calling (Phil. 3:13). I called every person involved to apologize for my attitude. Some relationships were restored; other people refused to speak to me. Nevertheless I had to do everything in my power to remove the hook from my heart. I knew that once I did, I would no longer be easy prey for the enemy's old tricks. I would be able to stride right past him and straight through the next mega door.

The adversarial traps that are set near your new open door are linked to past sins, hurts, offenses, doubts, and struggles. Shock the enemy by removing every hook. Forget what is behind and reach for what is ahead. Remove all hesitation. It zaps needed energy and is a sure sign that something from the past is still present.

Let me make another very important point about Jesus's warning: "For offenses must come, but woe to that man by whom the offense comes!" (Matt. 18:7). The words *must come* seem to imply that we *must* experience offense. That is far from the truth. "Must come" is *anagke* in the Greek. If we examine aspects of the word's meaning, we see that it refers to the means by which offense comes—essentially from needs imposed by the circumstances. Five words in the definition of *anagke* describe the circumstances specifically: custom, argument, calamity, distress, and straits.[5] In order for offense to take hold, these circumstances *must be* in play. Let's take a look.

Custom (and culture)

People are very protective of their customs and often get offended when their customs are not respected. Every family has its own customs and culture. When cultural lines are crossed, it creates relational tension. The remedy is the culture of honor, which is kingdom culture. It protects covenant relationships and fights against offense. If we are looking for the kingdom's culture, it will ward off the power of sin in our relationships.

Argument

Arguments are a great way to become offended. Dogmatic and judgmental people love to argue; others like to play the devil's advocate. Let me say this up front: the devil doesn't need anyone on his side.

Argumentative people have very few real relationships because the atmosphere around them is charged not with righteousness, peace, and joy in the Holy Spirit, but with frustration. The Holy Spirit is not argumentative; He is the bringer of joy. He is a comforter. Allow Him, the Spirit of truth, to rule every relationship.

Arguers are rarely honest about their weakness and tend to argue even when they are wrong. If we focus on the fact that we are all on the same team, we will withstand all opposition to the covenant relationship. Whether you are wrong or right, pursue peace.

Calamity

When people feel like everything in their lives goes wrong, they tend to be easily offended. Calamity produces a victim mentality, and victims are among the hardest people with whom to share a covenant relationship. Everything has to be about them. They are inwardly focused, they blame others for their failures, and they make excuses for everything. Often these are people who attract misfortune simply by the way they interact with others.

It reminds me of what children do when they touch a hot stove. They look around to see who hurt them, and the first person they see is the culprit. Children do not have the cognitive ability to understand that no one caused their hurt. They don't realize that their actions produced their pain.

My wife was three years old when she stuck a knitting needle into an electrical socket. She got shocked! Her first thought was that the man next door did something to her. For sixteen years she had bad thoughts about him. The worst part was that a few years later he ended up working at her school. Every day she had to deal with the strong, uncomfortable feelings she still had toward him.

The way to break this kind of cycle is to believe that good things happen to you. Goodness and mercy follow you all the days of your life, not calamity. You are blessed going in and coming out.

You are the head and not the tail. No weapon formed against you will prosper. You are free!

Distress

Distress is crippling. Distressed people are anxious, sad, depressed, and stressed out. They tend to be needy and clingy. Their stress causes them to be inwardly focused and self-preserving. Anxiety in a distressed person is heightened, causing them to have high-maintenance relationships. They live with foreboding about relationships, money, and opportunities. They tend to be so tense that they cause strife wherever they go.

Distress dissipates when we have the peace that passes understanding and keep our hearts and minds fixed on Christ Jesus.

Straits

When a person feels constricted they tend to push back, even if the constriction is not real. Straits are narrow places, including narrow mind-sets and narrow financial situations. People in straits tend to feel as though they don't control their worlds. Something or someone is the hindrance to their next level, and someone else is the key to their breakthrough.

Constricted people are often moochers and users. They are frequently those who need to be needed. They seek controlling relationships they feel they can govern. They have lost their ability to make reasonable decisions for themselves but are quick to make decisions for others. They are stunted both by being controlled and by being controlling. Whether they find themselves in straits or create them for themselves and others, straits are about lack, control, and restriction—all of which open doors of offense.

If we can overcome these hooks within our character and relationships, we can live free from offense. If we are free from offense, we will not step into the traps of the adversary. Offense must have one of these five hooks if it is to prevent you from reaching your open door.

IT'S TIME

We can remove all hooks by focusing on doing good. Galatians 6:9 says: "Let us not grow weary while doing good, for in due season we shall reap if we do not lose heart." We will not lose heart unless we get tired of looking for good things in negative circumstances.

It's about time! You will reach the door as long as you don't stop looking for it. Don't take your eyes off the huge opportunities that are coming your way. Don't trade them for small, temporary fixes and shortcuts. I promise you that your *megas* door is worth the wait. There is something beautiful, handsome, excellent, eminent, choice, surpassing, precious, useful, suitable, commendable, admirable, and magnificent coming in your appointed time—if you don't become utterly spiritless and worn out. (Consider that my amplified rendering of Galatians 6:9!)

Sarah's door was big. She waited a *long* time for it to open. Then some unexpected visitors stopped by with amazing news:

> They said to [Abraham], "Where is Sarah your wife?" And he said, "She is in the tent." The LORD said, "I will surely return to you about this time next year, and Sarah your wife shall have a son." And Sarah was listening at the tent door behind him.
> —GENESIS 18:9–10, ESV

Every promise has an appointed time. Sarah listened at the door to hear God reveal His plans. You can listen at the door of heaven and hear the promises of God for your life. Intimacy and closeness with Him will keep your vision clear. Sarah's vision needed clearing up. Until the visitors came, she believed she already had her promised child. She was wrong. Ishmael was not the promised child. Her Isaac was yet to come.

Sarah did not listen at the door to hear about the promise. She was curious about what God was up to and happened to hear

Him talking about her. She found out that there was yet another level about to open up!

Be curious about what God is talking about and less curious about what you want. You might find out that God is talking about what you want anyway. Do everything in your power to stay where God's voice is. Find it in the Word, in worship, and in prayer. Listen for His voice, and you will have the wisdom necessary for life and godliness.

If you feel as if your promise is stalled, just know that there is no better posture or preparation for your appointed time than to realize that it's not your time yet and you need to stay in God's presence until it is. Keep listening at the door. The presence and instruction of God will give you the upper hand and a keen sense of where you are.

God asked Abraham where his wife was. He replied, "She's in the tent." A note for husbands: Abraham knew where his wife was. It's our duty to be fully aware of our wives' emotional and spiritual conditions. We are the head of the house, but our wives are the heart. A healthy house needs a healthy heart. An isolated heart can lead to a "heart attack" in the family. That's my advice, free of charge.

Isolation is not God's will for anyone. The very reason God gave Adam a wife was so he would not be alone. Isolation is not the same as what we call a wilderness experience. God uses the latter. He has typically separated people to be alone with Him in preparation for promotion and a deeper relationship in Him. Wilderness experiences build up identity and purpose. Isolation does not build up identity; it conceals it.

Wherever we are in God's plan, timing is key and He chooses to keep it in His own control. When we desire to be promoted, we have to remember that promotion comes from the Lord. We incline ourselves to His ways and He does the promoting (Ps. 75:5-7). Timing is a promotion issue, and God Himself sets it as He chooses.

The enemy understands that our society is set up for us to want everything in our timing, under our control, and within our understanding. When this is not possible, we tend to take matters in our own hands. More often than not this leads to defeat, devastation, and more disappointment.

People who are disappointed with God usually find themselves in this state. They are like children who throw fits over a toy they will lose interest in moments or days after getting it. Children think they understand what's good for them. Their parents know better; they have seen this scene play out many times.

God is omniscience and omnipotence, He looks at our circumstances and makes sense out of them that we cannot. When we learn from Him that it is not yet our time, it quenches our frustration, jealousy, and envy.

TIME TO BE HUMBLE

When we become aware of what our time looks like, we also recognize what it doesn't look like. It takes humility to say, "It's not yet my time."

Jesus said it. He was humble, and Peter left us instructions to help us imitate His humility:

> Therefore humble yourselves under the mighty hand of God, that He may exalt you in due time, casting all your care upon Him, for He cares for you. Be sober, be vigilant; because your adversary the devil walks about like a roaring lion, seeking whom he may devour. Resist him, steadfast in the faith, knowing that the same sufferings are experienced by your brotherhood in the world.
> —1 PETER 5:6–9

God's mighty hand has three functions in our lives: it protects, provides, and promotes. When we humble ourselves under God's hand, He takes responsibility for us. The word *mighty* tells us specifically what we can expect. Humbling ourselves under

God's *mighty* hand causes God to shelter us, deal mightily with our enemy, and lift our heads. He is mighty enough to do all three, even though we don't deserve them.

One act of humility trumps all previous works. If we stay humble, we will be delivered *and* exalted at the proper time. Peter said we humble ourselves by casting our cares upon God, knowing that He cares for us. That is the greatest form of humility—to let God be our provider. As long as we keep our cares by providing for ourselves, God's mighty hand cannot fully release His provision.

One of the primary strategies of the enemy is to use our cares against us. Whichever care or problem we don't surrender to God's mighty hand will be the one Satan uses to distract us from the door of opportunity. We see this in verse 8 from 1 Peter 5: "Be sober, be vigilant; because your adversary the devil walks about like a roaring lion, seeking whom he may devour."

Casting your cares is both sober and vigilant. It removes all opportunity for the devil to devour you. The enemy will try to trick you into taking care of yourself. "Resist him, steadfast in the faith, knowing that the same sufferings are experienced by your brotherhood in the world" (v. 9). The enemy wants to intimidate and control you. Resist him to his face with your faith in God's care. The enemy will flee, and your resistance will help set others free.

Genesis 4:7 says something very important regarding the sin at the door: "If you do well, will you not be accepted? And if you do not do well, sin lies at the door. And its desire is for you, but you should rule over it." In Genesis chapter 4 sin crouches at the door, but in Revelation 3:20 Jesus stands at the door and knocks, desiring to come in and fellowship with us! What is sin doing at the door? Sin wants to have dominion over you and hinder your fellowship with Christ. You must overcome and rule it!

You are called to be an overcomer. Revelation 3:21 says that if you overcome as Jesus did, you will rule like He does. Perfect timing, mega doors, and being exalted are not the primary focus. The primary focus is to rule over what wants to rule over you.

It is time for a wrestling mind-set. Sin is trying to pin you, but you must escape, get the takedown, and maintain the dominant position. This is your time to rule over things that have dominated you for years. Once you have dominion over them, they will never distract you again. It's your time to be free. It's your time to be happy. It's your time to overcome. It's time for you to start living instead of dying. It's your time to thrive instead of survive.

It's about time!

Chapter 11

THAT'S RIDICULOUS

I often hear people say that life isn't fair and life is hard. I also know people who experience great difficulties in life but never adopt a "life is hard" mind-set. They seem to possess a fortitude and tenacity that propels them beyond their circumstances. They appear to be offended that anything or anyone would attempt to stand in their way. They see obstacles as small issues on the horizon of their destinies. Their faith in their purpose is huge and builds within them an audacity to face the odds. They refuse to be bullied by the giants, even in a world where bullying is at an all-time high.

Bullying is not new, and it's not just for kids. Bullying happens in schools, at work, and in churches. It's become the spirit of this age. A bully's purpose is to crush the confidence and dreams of those he bullies.

I love movies in which the bully victimizes his target one too many times. The victim thinks, "Enough is enough! What do I have to lose? I'm getting beat up already. I might as well fight back." The victim taps into the faith that was there all along. He just needed a big enough reason to break forth.

Do you suppose David's huge faith just happened in time for the battle with the Philistines? Goliath was not David's first encounter with a bully. He had been dealing with bullies throughout his formative years.

This tells me that a hard life is not meant to break us but to make us. A hero is not needed until there is a villain, and David knew some villains. Among them were a lion and a bear. David didn't simply fight these sheep killers, he also developed an audacious, huge faith from fighting them.

When David was king, he faced the fight of his life. Three armies were pursuing him when he said: "I would have fainted if I hadn't believed to see the goodness of the Lord in the land that I live in!" (See Psalm 27:13.) His faith may have started as a gift, but it was developed through hardship. David believed that God still had better days ahead for Him. God didn't raise him up as king to die as hunted prey.

You need to have the same fortitude. God didn't bring you this far just to forsake you. He promised He would never leave nor forsake you (Heb. 13:5).

God didn't make David a shepherd over a few sheep just because He needed someone to watch them. God had a bigger plan in play. When the bear and the lion arose to take his sheep, David said, "Not on my watch!"

David faced a choice. He would either become a victim or he would stand in faith against an opponent much larger and stronger than he was. Something rose up within David, and without hesitating he charged into the battle with the lion and the bear and defeated them (1 Sam. 17:37).

No Mere Man

When David arrived at the front line between Israel and the Philistines, he was just a young man running lunches to his brothers. When he saw the giant Goliath taunting and challenging the armies of God (1 Sam. 17), a sense of purpose arose within David, and he asked what was going on.

From within David came a faith that the whole army of Israel failed to display! At first King Saul questioned his ability to back up his words. But David's faith was convincing. He recounted to King Saul his previous victories over the lion and the bear. David explained that the giant would fall in the same manner as his previous foes.

King Saul recognized that David had an uncommon confidence, so he gave him permission to fight on behalf of Israel. The encounter that followed was epic!

> Then [David] took his staff in his hand; and he chose for himself five smooth stones from the brook, and put them in a shepherd's bag, in a pouch which he had, and his sling was in his hand. And he drew near to the Philistine. So the Philistine came, and began drawing near to David, and the man who bore the shield went before him. And when the Philistine looked about and saw David, *he disdained him*; for he was only a youth, ruddy and good-looking. So the Philistine said to David, "Am I a dog, that you come to me with sticks?" And the Philistine cursed David by his gods.
>
> —1 SAMUEL 17:40–43

The greatest weapon the enemy has is intimidation, by whatever means possible. Goliath thought he could intimidate David as he had intimidated the army of Israel. He tried talking down to David and belittling him. He *disdained* David, which means he showed his contempt for him. The strategy was supposed to make David believe that defeating Goliath was impossible. David refused to allow the giant to decide what could or could not happen. Instead, he followed Goliath's verbal attacks with a witty response of his own. David described how he would defeat Goliath in the power of God's covenant, and he reminded everyone how far outside that covenant Goliath was.

According to Mark 10:27 all things are possible if I am with God. Victory becomes impossible only when I act as a mere man. David was not merely a man. He was an anointed man in covenant with God. No matter how big Goliath was, he was just a man. And until he met David, he was accustomed to fighting only mere men.

Recently my wife woke up with a horrible pain in her back. Immediately the words, "That's impossible!" shot out of her mouth. She said the declaration was not intentional. It was as if the Holy Spirit Himself spoke out.

When she told me the story, I realized that we have allowed the enemy, our flesh, circumstances, and other limits to tell us what's impossible. Only God and His children can declare what's impossible. The devil doesn't have the authority to tell us what can or will be. For him to do that, he must be stronger than God and His children.

For years I have talked about the impossible, but I never took the time to study the definition of the word. *Impossible* means that you don't have enough strength to bring about the desired result.

OK. Are you doing something today that you once called impossible?

I am. I thought that it was impossible for me to write a book. Not any longer. I have gained the strength to do what I never thought could be done through me. You too are being prepared for the impossible. You might feel a certain limitation today, but through the power of God you will be strong enough to do it tomorrow. Don't give up. Every time you press against the limits, you gain more strength.

The enemy is not strong enough to stop you from growing. That's why he tries to scare you instead of overpower you. God thinks it is humorous for the enemy to try to withstand Him.

"He that sitteth in the heavens shall laugh: the LORD shall have them in derision" (Ps. 2:4, KJV).

The Lord is amused by His enemies. He sits on His throne of authority, laughing and making fun of them. The Lord shall have them in *derision,* which is "the act of laughing at in contempt…Contempt manifested by laughter; scorn…a laughing-stock."[1] The funniest part of this is that the enemy tries to do to us what God does to him. So what is his problem? Satan's major problem is that He doesn't have a throne of authority to sit on.

God laughs at him. Laughter is a response to what seems ridiculous. Ridicule is associated with contempt. *To ridicule* is to hold in "contemptuous laughter; laughter with some degree of contempt; derision."[2] Ridicule is aimed at what is not just laughable, but also improper, absurd, or despicable. Sacred subjects should never be treated with ridicule.

God thinks it is laughable, improper, absurd, and despicable to think the enemy would set himself against God. It is utterly ridiculous for him to oppose the One who sits on the throne. It is also ridiculous for the enemy to set himself against us, the ones who have received everything from the One who sits in heaven. I like that Psalm 2:4 doesn't say the Lord sits on the throne; it says, "He who sits in the heavens…" The New Testament says that we are seated in heavenly places (Eph. 2:6). So not only does the Lord laugh, but we also laugh from a heavenly perspective.

Part of what we receive from God is our strength, according to King David:

> To Him who rides on the heavens, the ancient heavens; He who sends out His voice, a mighty voice. Ascribe strength to God; His majesty is over Israel, and His strength is in the clouds. O God, You are awesome from Your sanctuaries; the God of Israel is He who gives strength and power to people. Blessed be God!
> —PSALM 68:33–35, MEV

When I was in high school I weighed 169 pounds. I saw guys working out in the weight room with 45-pound plates on the bench-pressing bar for a total of 135 pounds. I thought lifting 135 pounds was impossible!

Much later I had grown a lot but hadn't lifted weights in many years. I joined a gym and thought I would start with the same weight that I strained at in high school. I slipped under the bar and pushed against it. To my shock, it was very light. Then I placed 45-pound plates on each side and lifted easily. One hundred thirty-five pounds became my warm-up weight!

The Lord is your strength coach and you are no mere human. What was once impossible can be easily achieved because you have gained strength from God through your everyday fight of faith. In Him you are getting stronger every day.

AGAINST ALL ODDS

Now Abraham and Sarah were old, advanced in years. The way of women had ceased to be with Sarah. So Sarah laughed to herself, saying, "After I am worn out, and my lord is old, shall I have pleasure?"
—GENESIS 18:11–12, ESV

Sarah laughed because God's promise was against the odds. As Sarah did, we think certain situations are ridiculous. We believe the odds are stacked against us because we are too old, too late, too unskilled, too poor, too little, or lacking what's necessary to achieve the desired result.

Actually difficult odds create the best environment for growing our faith. Faith and laughter grow best in the same environment: out-of-the-ordinary circumstances. To function, faith needs circumstances that seem impossible or unrealistic. Faith is unnecessary if the odds are not against us.

Decades earlier the odds were not necessarily against Abraham and Sarah. It was not until she was past childbearing years that the odds went upside down. Sarah was now way past her time for children, and her body stopped producing years earlier. So did her husband's. Even Paul referred to Abraham as a man who was "as good as dead" (Rom. 4:19, ESV).

Faith contradicts norms. Reason wants everything to stay reasonable. When unreasonable, inexplicable things happen, reason can lead to a victim's mind-set. Faith and a victim mind-set cannot work together. Faith is a victorious mind-set. It anticipates something good happening. It thinks, "I don't know how or when, but God is good and something good is going to happen to me."

Words like these give voice to faith for the future. But other voices compete with them when we also give reason, fear, doubt, and every other emotion a voice. The voice of reason tries to convince us that we are out of our minds to believe we could overcome. We often expect miracles to happen under controlled circumstances, but they don't. Imperfect circumstances are the womb of miracles, and faith is the seed.

Believing is seeing. We must believe, not in what we see, but in what we hope to see. True believing is seeing good things coming from negative circumstances. Yet believing doesn't stop there. If we believe, we *must* speak it out. Silence equals agreement with our circumstances.

Be verbal about what you believe. I am not talking about calling up a friend or neighbor and telling them what you are believing for. I am talking about speaking to the mountain, the tree, and the waves in the sea, as Jesus did. I am talking about speaking to the circumstances, obstacles, and forces that are trying to disdain you. Go ahead and ridicule *them*.

Take charge of your destiny with your words. It's ridiculous to think that you will not have a breakthrough. It's ridiculous for you not to be healed. Disdain and ridicule the circumstances that try to belittle you, instead of being intimidated by them.

Your tongue sets the course of your life. Your body and life will follow your tongue wherever it leads. It's like a bit in the horses mouth or a rudder on a large ship fighting against the wind (James 3:3–5). It has the power to move you through the resistance.

Proverbs 18:21 says: "Death and life are in the power of the tongue." The word for power used in Hebrew is *yad,* meaning "a hand, the open hand (indicating power, means, direction, etc.)."[3]

My wife always declares that who we are today is a manifestation of our previously spoken words. We must understand the weightiness of our words. Death and life are in the hand of the tongue. The hand displays power, brings about means, and gives direction. Our mouths release power and authority into our circumstances. The direction of our future and the means for everything we hope for are in our mouths. James 3:4 says our tongue is the rudder of our vessel!

Our words are seeds of faith. Fear is faith in the worst that can happen. When we speak words of faith, it's faith in the best that is yet to come. Seeds grow in dirt. If we plant fear seeds into the negative circumstances of our lives, we grow harvests of disappointment. If we plant seeds of faith there instead, we will grow a harvest of good things. Our words will either agree with and confirm our problems or contradict and change them.

We are not typical, and we are not statistics. It's ridiculous to assume that we should fold under pressure.

Who cares about the odds? With the right things flowing from our mouths, we will overcome *any* obstacles. "A good man out of the good treasures of his heart brings forth good things" (Matt. 12:35). How does a good man do that? The same way God brought forth everything that He said was good.

God said…then it was…and it was good (Gen. 1). God is good. His words are good. If we meditate on His life-giving words, His love, and His liberty, we will speak and eat its fruit. If we meditate on a good God, that's who we will speak about and receive from.

Our past disappointments will want to have their say. Sarah's spoke loudly. She laughed several times at the goodness of God, and asked, "After I am worn out, and my lord is old, shall I have pleasure?"

God's promises always seem too good to be true. At first we laugh out of pure shock because what we are hearing seems abnormal or absurd. We don't laugh at things that make sense, but at things that don't make sense. If an arrogant celebrity fell on his face on TV, it might get a chuckle. But if a caring and loving individual fell, I doubt anyone would laugh.

Remember: when God asks you to believe for something you have never seen before, He is setting you up for a higher level of faith than you have ever known. It's the favor of God, the goodness of God that draws you into levels not previously experienced. Getting there takes faith against all faith and hope against all hope. (See Romans 4:18.)

What matters is what you are willing to believe. So God asked Sarah a question that must have shocked her to the core. I know that coming from Him, it would have rocked me: "Is anything too hard for the LORD?" (Gen. 18:14.)

If you think *anything* is too hard for God, you must, I repeat, *must* build a bigger picture of Him in your heart and mind until He is so big that nothing is impossible for Him.

Is anything stronger than God? Is anything harder than the things God has done, such as creating the universe, for example? Make God bigger, stronger, harder, and better than everything else. If God is like a man, then you and I are hopeless. He *must* be good, and He *must* be big enough for us to have a faith that can surpass all understanding, circumstances, and experiences. This faith comes only from reading, quoting, meditating on, and rehearsing God's words every day, as often as we can.

You know some of my story. I once lived in disappointment, accusing God with questions such as "Why didn't You?" and "Why *did* You?" It was hard for me to rejoice when He blessed others because I did not feel blessed. Through my disappointment I saw Him as being unfair.

Mind you, I was in ministry at the time, preaching about God's goodness and wondering why He wasn't good to me. I did not realize how deeply disappointment had affected me. I remember hearing the Holy Spirit's voice clearly one day. He said, "Tracey, you are trying to stockpile millions of dollars, but I want you to stockpile faith."

Years before that I had received several promises from the Lord. One was to have wealth for the work of God. So every time we faced financial issues, it came down to the promise not yet being fulfilled. I took the issue into my own hands and worked on a plan to make millions for the gospel.

The harder I worked, the harder "I" worked. My faith went into getting the money and not into believing God. Every day I heard the enemy laughing at me. I had huge vision but not the money to achieve it. I felt ridiculed as I preached God's goodness and questioned His goodness for me.

I want to tell you something: you might feel ridiculed and disdained by the enemy, but it's not the end of your story.

A couple of years before I had this experience, Oral Roberts prayed over my wife and me, and we asked for the healing anointing. He prayed: "God, give these people the ability to believe You."

I thought to myself, "No, I asked for miracle-working power." I prayed silently to God, "Tell him to say miracle-working power!"

All he prayed for was the ability to believe God. I was blessed to have him pray for me, but as I walked away I was still stuck on "miracle-working power." I totally missed the fact that all the miracles, healing, and the building of a hospital and university came out of Oral Roberts's ability to believe God.

JUST *BELIEVE* ME!

A couple of years later I had a revelation of what really happened to me. While I was at a Billye Brim prayer conference in Branson, Missiouri, I woke up in the middle of the night and heard these words loud and clear: "*I am just trying to get you to believe Me!*"

That got my attention. I finally realized that it wasn't about my doing anything more than believing God. My faith in God would give Him the room He needed to show Himself good in my life!

So I made up my mind that God was good, no matter what was taking place. I began to meditate only on those things that are lovely, pure, and of a good report (Phil. 4:8). I listened to and read only things that built faith and hope. I did it every day!

God gave me this verse: "I believe that I shall look upon the goodness of the LORD in the land of the living!" (Ps. 27:13, ESV). Building faith and believing God became my focus. First I needed to believe in His goodness. If I couldn't believe that about Him, then I could not have the faith to see His goodness manifested.

The question God asked Sarah was about God's "bigness" and goodness. "Is anything too hard for God?" (Gen. 18:14). Sarah had to deal with what she believed. If she believed that He was big enough, there would be only one more question: "Is He good enough?"

We often base our ability to receive on *our* bigness and goodness. This is a form of works and sin consciousness. God has given us "all things that pertain to life and godliness" (2 Pet. 1:3). What do we bring to the table? The Bible says that God has given each one of us a supply of faith (Rom. 12:3). If we can believe that God is both big and good, then nothing is impossible, *because* we believe Him.

Let's look at Genesis 18:10 again:

> The LORD said, "I will surely return to you about this
> time next year, and Sarah your wife shall have a son."

And Sarah was listening at the tent door behind him.
Now Abraham and Sarah were old, advanced in years.
The way of women had ceased to be with Sarah. So
Sarah laughed to herself, saying, "After I am worn out,
and my lord is old, shall I have pleasure?"
                                        —GENESIS 18:10–12, ESV

The facts of Sarah's life—that she was advanced in years and
was beyond the "way of women"—were strong natural arguments
for her *not* to believe. Those facts tried to choke out the truth. The
truth was that God had made up His mind to return in a year
so Sarah would have a baby. The Holy Spirit is the Spirit of truth.
His desire is to contradict the facts (Sarah was old) with spiritual
truth and reality (God promised). If we insist on believing that
our dream is too big for God, we will forfeit His supernatural
participation and make the dream naturally impossible.

Years ago I heard the president of a well-known Christian television station preach. As I listened I heard in my spirit, "I will
give you a TV channel."

I thought to myself, "That's cool!"

It has never been my dream to have a television channel.
Needless to say, I started to dream about what it could look
like. I dreamed of a channel for indie filmmakers and musi-
cians and sound stages and film lots. I explored what it would be
like to executive produce films and music projects. I envisioned
becoming a distribution platform for young artists.

The vision was huge and consumed my thoughts. It was so big
that I started thinking I ought to break it into smaller portions.
I though it would have been good if I had broken it down into
phases. Instead, I created a single phase that I thought would be
an easy start. I shrunk God's dream to match my resources and
abilities!

Soon I became frustrated with the project, which I named
Destiny Channel. I eventually lowered the startup cost of the
channel to five figures, which was way below the original estimate.

My wife arranged for us to go on a family vacation to Las Vegas. I like going there because a lot of dreaming and big vision goes into the hotels. We checked into the MGM Signature Grand, a family-friendly hotel. The room was spectacular. When I opened the curtains to see the view, I realized it overlooked the MGM film lot.

Immediately I heard the Spirit say, "That's what I want. Don't shrink My dream. If you shrink My dream, thousands of dollars will be more difficult to raise than millions."

There was only one reason I had lowered the original vision; it was because of past disappointments. I tried (wrongly) to shrink down the dream to make it easier on myself and on God.

Here is my best advice: don't let past disappointments force current opportunities to make sense. Do *not* shrink the dream to make it easier on yourself. Especially don't try to make it easier for God. Keep it ridiculous! Don't laugh at the absurdly big vision. Rather, expect it to be unbelievably big.

Both disappointment and faith have something to say about your past experiences and current circumstances. In the beginning of Genesis 18:12 we read that "Sarah laughed to herself, saying…" (ESV). What have you been saying to yourself? Whatever you tell yourself today is already directing your future.

Have you ever noticed how hard it is to be negative in silence? Negativity and complaining always want to make their way out of our mouths. We often say, "I just have to say it."

My question is, "Why? Why do you have to say it?"

It's because whatever is in your heart proceeds out of your mouth. Sarah was only saying what she had already meditated on. You might be thinking, "What do you mean? Sarah didn't have a clue that this option was coming."

This is true, but without a doubt there was a reference to the past lodged somewhere in her heart. It said, "Others have had the pleasure of a child, but I guess I won't have it."

Can you see why Sarah's first response wasn't "Wow. That is exciting!"

No. She heard amazing news and said, "After I am worn out, and my lord is old, shall I have pleasure?" Her question stems from previous meditations of the heart. It was funny to Sarah to think that after all the years that had passed by, she would get pregnant and have a son.

In the late 1990s my wife and I were full-time itinerate ministers. We traveled to churches, youth ministries, retreats, and conferences. We taught the Word and ministered insight and restoration through the power of the Holy Spirit.

Here's what I mean by ministering insight. Have you ever had an image flash in your mind that you knew was not simply your imagination? That is the kind of insight I'm talking about. The Bible calls these flashes *words of knowledge.* In our ministry insight would precede the Holy Spirit restoring people physically, emotional, financially, relationally, etc. The Bible uses the term *healing* for restoration. In a nutshell this is how God would use us.

We were invited to preach at a youth camp for a young couple named Jonathan and Raydeane Owens in Idaho. My wife and I had met them only once before they picked us up at the airport and took us to lunch. While eating, I experienced one of those flashes of insight from God. I saw that Raydeane had breast cancer. I didn't feel the freedom to address it right then and there, but I knew that God wanted me to pray for her.

Later that evening in the service, I felt the freedom to share with her what I saw. It was true! She had been diagnosed with a cancerous lump. In His goodness God gave me a message for her. He told her to have three tests done and that the third test would be clear. She had already had one. She was scheduled for the second. So we prayed, finished the services, and went home. There was no physical sign of change.

A few weeks later I received a phone call from Jonathan. He asked, "How sure are you about the instruction from the Lord?"

I responded, "I am confident, but I will pray again."

He said, "The doctor is upset. He thinks we're being irresponsible. He had the nurse come in to talk to Raydeane because he thinks she's in shock. Raydeane keeps laughing and asking for a third test."

The doctor wanted to perform a procedure immediately. He actually told Raydeane that he was her only help. Raydeane was laughing because she had no doubt that God was going to be good to her. It was ridiculous for her to have any fear. It was ridiculous for the enemy to disdain her and try to ridicule her for believing in God's goodness.

Raydeane's confidence was so apparent that the nurse recognized her faith and was encouraged by it. The doctor finally gave in to ordering a third test. He was so mad that he said, "The results will be the same!"

A few days later the doctor called with the results. Raydeane was clear of cancer; it was removed miraculously by a good God! Raydeane and God had a great laugh.

You might not have an inspired prophetic word to trust in, but you do have the inspired Word of God to trust. No matter whether you have a prophetic word or the written Word, God's Word is what you must believe.

THE WORD TO STAND ON

David stood toe to toe with Goliath because of a word from God. David was destined to be king and the giant was both his obstacle and his opportunity. Without Goliath, David wouldn't have the chance to be king. Defeating Goliath was his only way into the royal family. David was Saul's personal musician, but that didn't get him nearer to the throne. Taking on the giant was his ticket.

If the Philistines won the battle, the kingdom would be lost. David had more to lose in the battle than anyone, and the odds were against him. His brother mocked him and accused him of pride. His leader underestimated him. Goliath cursed him and his God and ridiculed him. The deck was stacked against David.

Yet David was amused by Goliath. Read the account for yourself with that in mind:

> The Philistine said to David, "Come to me, and I will give your flesh to the birds of the heavens and to the beasts of the field."
>
> Then David said to the Philistine, "You come to me with a sword, a spear, and a shield, but I come to you in the name of the LORD of Hosts, the God of the armies of Israel, whom you have reviled. This day will the LORD deliver you into my hand. And I will strike you down and cut off your head. Then I will give the corpses of the Philistine camp this day to the birds of the air and to the beasts of the earth so that all the earth may know that there is a God in Israel. And then all this assembly will know that it is not by sword and spear that the LORD saves. For the battle belongs to the LORD, and He will give you into our hands."
>
> When the Philistine arose and came near to meet David, David hurried and ran toward the battle line to meet the Philistine. David put his hand in his bag and took from there a stone. And he slung it and struck the Philistine in his forehead. Therefore the stone sunk into his forehead and he fell upon his face to the ground.
>
> So David prevailed over the Philistine with a sling and with a stone. And he struck down the Philistine and slew him, but there was no sword in the hand of David.
>
> Therefore David ran and stood over the Philistine. Then he took his sword and drew it from out of its sheath, and he finished him off and he cut off his head with it.
>
> When the Philistines saw their champion was dead, they fled.
>
> —1 SAMUEL 17:44–51, MEV

I love it! I can see God on the throne laughing. And I see David smirking and chuckling as he says, "Then all this assembly shall know that the LORD does not save with sword and spear; for the battle is the LORD's, and He will give you into our hands."

Have you ever been so mad that you just started laughing? David didn't flinch! He didn't crumble under the ridicule of the giant. He ridiculed the giant right back. He didn't retreat when the giant started charging. David charged the giant with absolute faith and confidence in the promise of a future kingdom. It didn't matter who stood before him. He knew that he would be king.

David took the ridicule to another level. The giant had powerful weapons; all David had was the name of the Lord and a slingshot.

If all you have is a slingshot and the name of the Lord God, you can change the world. If all you have is a few dollars and the name of the Lord, you can do something great. If all you have is the name of the Lord, you can make history.

David didn't even have a sword to finalize the victory; David had to use Goliath's own sword to remove his head. If that is not ridiculous, I don't know what is. The Philistine army was so humiliated that they fled.

Today is the day that you will pick yourself up. Point your finger at the obstacles in your life. Fill your mouth with God's promises. Know that you are anointed for the job. Laugh at the opposition and refuse to back down. Defeating your biggest challenge is the only way to achieve your destiny. Your giant is both your obstacle and your opportunity. Stare it down and laugh it to shame. Ridicule it in faith knowing that the God of heaven will give you strength to do the impossible.

It's ridiculous that it would have victory in your life. If God is for you, who can be against you? Is anything too hard for the Lord?

Chapter 12

IT'S TOO HARD

As a pastor, father, and success and results coach I often hear people say, "It's too hard!"

When this claim is part of your everyday speech, you are unknowingly building subconscious tension and sabotaging your success.

If you tell yourself that you can't do something, your brain will lock onto the impossibility of it and keep you from achieving it. The same effect occurs when we approach any endeavor with the idea that it's going to be hard. No one wants to run against hard. Hard rocks hurt me as a child. The ground was hard when I fell off of my bike. The wall was hard when I ran into it.

The surfaces I described are hard. Come into sudden contact with them and pain will be the response. Therefore the word *hard* will always be associated with pain, even if the "hard thing" is in the future.

Trade the word *hard* for *challenging*. *Challenging* makes it clear that the task will take a lot of strength and energy, but it will not be impossible.

I honor Mary, the mother of Jesus. Her response to the impossible was, "It's going to be a challenge, but it's not hard." Even her response to the angel was unique. Notice the exchange:

> And having come in, the angel said to her, "Rejoice, highly favored one, the Lord is with you; blessed are you among women!" But when she saw him, *she was troubled at his saying*, and considered what manner of greeting this was.
> —LUKE 1:28–29

When angels appear in the Bible, the usual response is shock at the sight of them. However, Mary seemed to be more amazed by what the angel said. She was more interested in the idea that she was highly favored and blessed among women than she was curious about how the angel looked. I just love Mary's confidence and boldness!

The angel shared the most astounding news that a teenage girl in Israel could hear—she was going to be the mother of the Messiah. Luke 1:34 speaks of a young lady with nerves of steel. Her response was both steady and intelligent: "How can this be, since I do not know a man?"

The angel's response was, "The Holy Spirit will come upon you, and the power of the Highest will overshadow you" (v. 35). The angel continued to build Mary's faith by testifying of her cousin Elizabeth's miraculous pregnancy. The angel finished the conversation saying: "For with God nothing will be impossible" (v. 37).

Mary was handed the key to the impossible: *impossible things happen when the Holy Spirit comes upon you!* When He comes upon your natural, He makes it supernatural and uncommon. The uncommon visions and purposes God sets for our lives cannot be accomplished through natural means. The dreams He gives require help from the Holy Spirit.

The more uncommon, wonderful, and extraordinary your purpose, the more uncommon, wonderful, and extraordinary your reliance on God must be. We can do the impossible only with God's help. Through the power of the Holy Spirit, God will give us the strength to do what we couldn't do before.

Too Good to Be True

Sarah would not admit that she laughed at the Lord's goodness. God's desire was never to punish her anyway, but only to cause her to believe He was good. So instead of rebuking her, He gave her an unbelievable promise: "Is anything too hard for the LORD? At the appointed time I will return to you, about this time next year, and Sarah shall have a son" (Gen. 18:14, ESV).

Sarah had been through a lot by that time. But God is good! He had to be better than everything she had previously experienced, simply because He *is* good.

In the end the challenges you face must produce a benefit equal to or bigger than the problem. Nothing can be harder than He is good. Nothing can be harder than God. Let me explain: the word *hard* in the Hebrew means, "to be marvelous, be wonderful, be surpassing, be extraordinary, separate by distinguishing action…to be beyond one's power, be difficult to do, to be difficult to understand, to be wonderful, be extraordinary."[1]

Is anything more marvelous, wonderful, surpassing, extraordinary, distinguishing in action, powerful, difficult, difficult to understand, wonderful, or extraordinary than the Lord? Of course not! God is harder than anything that would try to impose its power and authority on you.

A natural man believes that things are possible based upon his previous references, testimonies, or experiences. The spiritual man believes that something is possible through believing that God can do what no one else can.

God does impossible things. The natural man might believe that God can do it but feels it is unlikely based upon previous experience. The spiritual man has a belief in God and His abilities, even though there is no previous reference for Him. For instance, sages say that Abraham started his search for God at three years of age, yet God didn't reveal Himself to Abraham until he was seventy-five years old.

Abraham continued in logical assent to God for seventy-two years. Once God revealed Himself, there was no turning back for Abraham. When it came time to believe that God could and would give him a child at one hundred years of age, Abraham believed God, even though he had never seen an old couple have a child. Over time Abraham developed the faith muscles that allowed him to believe God for what seemed impossible.

Our five senses make believing hard. The more we rely on the spirit life, the more we trust in the unseen and believe that nothing is too hard for the Lord. When we trust in God more than what we see, we tap into His creative power.

In a single verse the prophet Jeremiah showed us how the world really works: "Ah Lord GOD! behold, thou hast made the heaven and the earth by thy great power and stretched out arm, and there is nothing too hard for thee" (Jer. 32:17, KJV).

If God has made everything with His great power and outstretched arm, couldn't He easily manipulate what He has made to solve any problem that you have? God's outstretched arm made it; He should be able to fix it. God fixes things all the time. He gives us wisdom. He gives us insight. He gives us comfort. He still performs miracles.

In Boston a woman diagnosed with diabetes received prayer during a healing and miracle service. She went to the bathroom to check her blood sugar and it was completely normal. The meetings lasted for a couple weeks in several different venues in the area. After a few days the woman gave her testimony but kept saying, "I don't believe it!"

Even though the proof was in her blood sugar test (which had been perfect every day), the healing was stunning to her. God wants to do things that are too good to be true. When the woman said, "I don't believe it!" she wasn't really questioning God. What she was really saying was, "It's too good to be true!"

When God does something that is too hard for anyone else to do, it will leave people speechless. You are called to do things that require God's outstretched arm. You are called to experience God's goodness to the level that it is shocking and too good to be true.

Our lives should testify that nothing is too hard for the Lord. We cannot look at life with our abilities in mind, but with God's abilities in mind. Faith puts pressure on God, not us!

HIS KINGDOM WITHIN YOU

God does the work, but His kingdom authority and rule is in every believer:

> Now when [Jesus] was asked by the Pharisees when the kingdom of God would come, He answered them and said, "The kingdom of God does not come with observation; nor will they say, 'See here!' or 'See there!' For indeed, the kingdom of God is within you."
>
> —LUKE 17:20–21

There is no force greater than the kingdom of God. Have you ever thought about why the enemy works so hard to mess up your world? It's because God is moving right in your midst. He is not coming from "out there" somewhere. He is coming from within you. He inserted His creative force, His judicial authority, and eternal faith inside you. As you look outward for a breakthrough, the answers to all your prayers are inside you. The kingdom doesn't come with observation, it comes from within. That's why we must participate with God as He brings about the miracle. It's not about watching things happen; it's about the overshadowing of the Holy Spirit that makes them happen. The kingdom is within you, and the Holy Spirit is upon you. The kingdom of God is righteousness, peace, and joy in the Holy

Spirit (Rom. 14:17). God's kingdom rules from within through the power that is upon you.

You are harder than anything that can come your way. The key is not to trust in what you see, but to seek to create what you hope to see. It is not enough for God to be amazing; we must be amazing also. He has given us His power to do it.

God needed someone on the earth to agree with Him, so, He gave us the power to agree: He put His kingdom within us so we could agree with His outstanding abilities. He made us righteous so we could agree with His righteousness. He gave us faith so we could agree with His unwavering faith. He put everything that He is inside of us so that we could agree with Him.

Psalm 42:7 says it this way: *"Deep calls unto deep at the noise of Your waterfalls; all Your waves and billows have gone over me."* God needs depth in you to reflect the deep in Him. God needs the wonder in you to match the wonder in Him. If God is extraordinary, He needs you and me to exhibit extraordinary faith like His. As sons and daughters of God we need to represent Him.

Jesus came to earth as God's Son sent to love people. God loved the world so much, He gave His son for it (John 3:16). The origin of the word translated "loved" in John 3:16 does not point to an emotion but a decision, suggesting a clear choice. God's decision to love mankind was because He believed in what we could become. You could say, "God so believed in the world that He gave His Son."

Modern society uses the word *love* so freely that it has lost much of its power. Yet believing in someone is universally powerful. Test it. Find someone and tell them that you believe in them. Those few words will get their attention and will prompt a question: "Why?" In other words, they will want to hear more.

If you say, "I love you!" the response will be simple: "I love you too!" or "Thank you!" Some might ask, "Why?" but for a different reason than when you express faith in them.

The Lord came to set us free by His love. His love for us has also prepared unimaginably good things for us according to 1 Corinthians 2:9: "But, as it is written, 'What no eye has seen, nor ear heard, nor the heart of man imagined, what God has prepared for those who love him'" (ESV).

It is exciting to know that God has prepared things for us that no one has ever seen, heard of, or imagined. These things are so uniquely ours that they have never been shared with anyone else except with the Holy Spirit.

Things are prepared for you that only God's imagination could form. They are so amazing and rare that only the Holy Spirit can help you see and receive them. They can only be known by searching out the Holy Spirit. First Corinthians 2:10 says that only the Holy Spirit knows everything: "These things God has revealed to us through the Spirit. For the Spirit searches everything, even the depths of God" (ESV).

When symptoms pop up, the natural man runs to Google, but the spiritual man runs to God. The Spirit of God is a much better resource, but we must have faith if we are going to ask for wisdom from Him (James 1:5–6).

The Holy Spirit will search as deeply as you are curious. If you lack curiosity about the deep things of God, He has nothing to work with. Curiosity causes you to desire understanding. It is a form of faith.

Here's what I mean: The natural man seeks to understand before he believes. The spiritual man believes and then asks the Holy Spirit for understanding. The natural man is caught in a conundrum: he doesn't understand because he insists on understanding the truth before he accepts it. The spiritual man accepts the truth from God's Word by faith before he completely understands it, and receives understanding.

One of my life's goals is to get my pilot's license. There are many levels of skill needed to pilot a plane safely. One is to be able to fly by instruments alone. Some years ago now we heard the news that John F. Kennedy Jr., his wife, and sister-in-law were killed in a plane crash. Some speculated that he had not finished his instrument-flying training. Because of the conditions at the time of the accident, Kennedy needed to fly by his instruments rather than by sight. The weather deprived him of clear visual cues; instruments alone could guide him.

In life our view is often obstructed by circumstances. At those times we should be able to fly by instruments only. When we cannot see where we are going, the Holy Spirit will lead us into the things that have been prepared for us. If we are going to live in faith, we don't need our natural eyes or ears to do the job. Faith is not based upon observation but on the kingdom from within.

LOVE ABOVE ALL

GOD HAS GIVEN us His kingdom because He loves us. Now we choose to have faith in His love.

> To know the love of Christ which surpasses knowledge; that you may be filled with all the fullness of God. Now to Him who is able to do exceedingly abundantly beyond all that we ask or imagine, according to the power that works in us, to Him be the glory.
> —EPHESIANS 3:19–21, MEV

We know God has prepared great things for us, but we can't always wrap our minds around the idea. He desires to do more than what we could ask or think.

Wait! I thought that in order to have faith we must be able to both see it, think about it, and meditate on it. That is true, but Ephesians 3 tells us that we should also believe for things that we have never seen nor heard. The only way that can happen is if we stop believing for things and simply believe God. Then our energy goes into believing that He exists and He rewards us for diligently seeking Him.

If God asks us to believe for a child at a ripe old age, we won't wonder how or when it will happen. We will simply believe that *it will* happen. There are things God desires to do that our minds cannot comprehend. The only way He can get those things to us or through us is by our believing Him.

Eyes to see and ears to hear—that's how I would describe spiritual discernment. We walk by faith and not by sight (2 Cor. 5:7). By faith all things were brought into existence from the invisible (Heb. 11:3). *To discern* means "to perceive by the sight or some other sense or by intellect."[2] Spiritual people never rely on their faculties to gain understanding or make a judgment. The just live by faith (Rom. 1:17). The mind of Christ (which we have) is a mind settled on living by faith and not by visual cues. Jesus never trusted His eyes or ears. He trusted what His Father revealed (John 5:19).

The Lord revealed to Sarah that her promise was a year away (Gen. 18:14), helping her to discover a fresh fervor for the promise. God wants to confirm that He is with you and your promise is still on its way. Lay aside disappointment. Wait on Him and He will renew your strength like that of an eagle (Isa. 40:31). Let God set your expectation. Expect Him to be good as He sets the direction for your life.

God is stronger than anything you are up against. Nothing is too wonderful for the Lord.

Chapter 13

HONEST TO GOD

As a child I remember the surge of energy that would flow through my body whenever I was asked about something I had done wrong.

"Why didn't you clean your room?" asked Mom.

"I did!" I replied, as my adrenalin surged.

My answer did not hold water. The floor was covered with clothing I had worn days earlier. I clearly had not cleaned my room.

We have all heard excuses such as "The dog ate my homework!" or "I didn't eat it. So-and-so ate it!" These excuses are lies in disguise. As a society we have learned to avoid getting into trouble. The approach is so widespread that we would rather lie or run to escape the consequences.

Why would a person lie to your face when the evidence against them is so blatant? The rationale is this: they believe they can keep the lie going and stay out of trouble, at least a little longer.

Years ago we had a man in our ministry who was a rep for an equipment manufacturer. When we needed equipment he said he could order it through his company. So we made the purchase through them.

Months passed and the equipment still had not arrived. When we asked about it, he said it was backordered and would be coming soon. A few more months went by. I called him into the office and asked again about the order. I had a strong suspicion that something wrong was going on. He would not admit it but offered another believable excuse to buy himself more time.

Finally I called the company myself. It was just as I suspected! They said the equipment line was no longer on backorder and had been shipping for the past few months. I became angry at the news.

I called the gentlemen in again and gave him a chance to be honest. He declined, so I told him I had called the manufacturer directly. He repeated his previous excuse, and I told him what his company told me: the items were not on backorder.

I asked him, "What happened to the money?"

He tried another excuse and then blamed someone else. When he realized he was caught, he admitted taking the money because he was behind on his bills. Once he told the truth, each of his previous excuses was moved into the category called *lies*. The situation was unpleasant, but once he became honest, there was opportunity for restoration. Regret, repentance, and then respect made room for mercy.

The man was afraid of getting into trouble, but not because he'd ever been in trouble with me. He obviously had experienced enough trouble in his past to trigger a fight-or-flight response. This was what motivated him to keep lying. Trouble and disappointment are fast partners with fear, and fear is the primary motivation for denial.

People who have been disappointed don't want to get into trouble. They know it brings additional grief and disappointment, and they will do almost anything to avoid that. Unhealthy choices and responses serve only to temporarily conceal the problem. In traumatic or tragic situations fear can act as a coping mechanism. Dishonesty is denial of the truth. These are not healthy approaches, but to the person in trouble they seem better than the alternatives.

In *How to Win Friends and Influence People* Dale Carnegie talks about a doctor who believed that it is better for some who have lost their minds to stay in that state because they have found a relatively happy place to live. That sounds shocking, I know. We certainly don't want people to lose their minds. Yet I understand Carnegie's point, and I see a parallel: dishonesty is a form of insanity. A person temporarily lets go of reality in order to continue the lie, *knowing* it is a lie and knowing it could eventually be uncovered. It is the troubled person's temporary happy place. But notice that I said temporary. Unlike that doctor, I do not believe this is a place people should remain.

In Sarah's case I am *not* saying that she was insane; I am saying that she resorted to denial. "But Sarah denied it, saying, 'I did not laugh,' for she was afraid. He said, 'No, but you did laugh'" (Gen. 18:15, ESV).

Sarah laughed. She knew it and God knew it. Abraham might have known it too. Yet she flat out denied it. She did not want to get in trouble. I believe disappointment predisposed her to doing this. We rarely discuss the pain Sarah went through to share her husband with Hagar. How challenging it must have been to co-raise Ishmael. Imagine the pain she felt when her servant turned on her. I suspect Sarah had many tough days.

There was also the temporary relief in knowing that at least Abraham had his heir. But then after thirteen years God said, "Let's restart the clock. Ishmael is not the child I promised."

The one thing that seemed settled in Sarah's mind was now back in play. The problem she had "fixed" was now "rebroken." So Sarah laughed, but God heard her.

The dictionary definition of disappoint is "to fail to fulfill the expectations or wishes of."[1] Sarah exhibited signs of disappointment by laughing at the goodness of God. Had He visited her forty years earlier, she would not have laughed at His promise. But she had since experienced many painful things.

It is bizarre to think that we can react to something in the present without realizing that we are actually responding to a previous circumstance—and it is still affecting our judgment!

As I said earlier, when I was commissioned by God to write this book, I was completely oblivious to any personal disappointment. I was also unaware of the paralyzing impact that it was having on my effectiveness and confidence regarding my destiny. I am thankful that God revealed it!

MOVING BEYOND LOSS

Sarah's laugh was one thing; her outright denial was another. Denial is a clear sign of disappointment. Sarah refused to believe that her laugh signaled doubt. According to ancient Jewish wisdom, she thought that she laughed from joy just as her husband Abraham had. The reality is that because of a history of disappointment, she did not really believe the miracle would or could happen. Her heart deceived her (as ours often do) because she was struggling to believe God.

Sarah *denied* that she laughed. The Hebrew word means, "to be untrue, in word (to lie, feign, disown) or deed (to disappoint, fail, cringe)—deceive, deny, dissemble, fail, deal falsely, be found liars, (be-)lie, lying."[2] I find "the deed to disappoint" an interesting part of *denied*. Fortunately for Sarah God's love meant He could never be disappointed. Yet her actions would likely have disappointed most mortals.

Sarah tried to cover over where she really was. When we say we are OK, but our body responses say otherwise, our symptoms—laughing, crying, sweating, hot flashes, hair loss, hives, loss of appetite, being red-faced—indicate that our emotions are communicating with our bodies, but our conscious minds are not getting the message.

Remember that there are two kinds of disappointed people: those who recognize their disappointment and those who manage to deny it even to themselves. I made the second group. I became a great projector of future opportunities, and through excuse making, a denier of past failures. My biochemistry always gave me away, however. I love how God handled Sarah's disappointment. He simply overrode it with a greater promise than the first one. This new promise worked in her for a year, rebuilding her faith and focus. Instead of harping on the denial problem, God made her full of faith, fully focused, and fully expecting good things from Him. He focused Sarah on the future rather than the past so she could move on from disappointment.

God put such a short time frame on the breakthrough that Sarah had to get over her past. She had a lot to do to be ready for what was coming. Pressing on to the next level is a key to healing disappointment. The next level demands attention and energy that can no longer be squandered on old hurts.

God was good to give Sarah something else to believe in and a set time in which to see His faithfulness fulfilled. Faith and disappointment both involve expectation. Faith expects good things; disappointment expects things to go wrong. Faith expects God to be good; disappointment has a difficult time believing Him.

My wife and I experienced loss as a young married couple. No matter what you have heard, miscarriage is hard. There is a lot of disappointment associated with the experience. It challenged our faith in a good God. Loving people tried their best to encourage us, but the pain remained. We even started experiencing a little fear each month when we did pregnancy tests.

The issue did not budge until the Lord spoke so lovingly to our hearts: "You will never experience loss like that again!" His comfort is amazing. His words were enough to start building our faith in His goodness again, but the full healing came when we held our baby boy. All the anger, disappointment, and fear left when we beheld the Lord's blessing.

HONESTY

Honesty is the best way to prepare for the future. God will speak about your future to get you to be honest about where you are. Peter learned this the hard way after promising Jesus that he would be willing to die for Him: "Lord, why can I not follow You now? I will lay down my life for Your sake" (John 13:37).

Jesus had a very clear picture of Peter's future. He knew that Peter would deny knowing Him before he would die with Him. In John 13:38 Jesus probed Peter's heart again for honesty: "Will you lay down your life for My sake? Most assuredly, I say to you, the rooster shall not crow till you have denied Me three times."

Peter was so determined to go with Jesus that he made a promise he could not keep. Going with Jesus was not the subject; the new commandment of love was the subject. Jesus spoke briefly about leaving, but His larger point was the love walk for His followers.

Love is a key part of honesty. When love is involved, there is no room for fear or denial. To clarify, there is a difference between the fear of God and being frightened of God. The fear of God understands that God is holy yet trustworthy, dependable, and full of love. Those who understand this love have the desire to repent; they want their thoughts and ways to match God's. Those who are afraid of God misunderstand His love and His goodness.

The genuine fear of God is the starting point of wisdom and knowledge. The love of God keeps us honest with Him and ourselves. During my time of despair I found myself praying inappropriate prayers, which I now call dishonest prayers. If God had answered them, He would have done me more harm than good. My prayer life was motivated by pride; I projected myself further along in my development than I really was. Pride made my prayers self-serving; I lacked the capacity to maintain what I was asking Him to do.

I was like a three-year-old asking to drive a car. Children that age cannot handle cars. Given the keys and assuming they could slip them into the ignition, they most likely could not turn on the engine. Nor would they be able to see over the dashboard. They would not be able to steer properly or reach the gas or brake pedals.

What good would car keys do for three-year-olds? None. They would simply frustrate and endanger them.

It wasn't until God showed me what I was projecting in my prayers that I realized why some of my prayers went unanswered. Let's assume my life was a line starting at zero and ending at the one hundred mark. I was praying prayers as though I had made the fifty mark and was believing God for sixty-five-mark break-throughs. I was reaching forward, which was good. But until the Lord opened my eyes, I had no idea that I was actually parked at number twenty-five.

Pride had distorted my view. If God had answered my sixty-five-mark prayers, I would have suffered damage. In not answering my sixty-five-mark requests, God was saving me from myself. Had I been honest with Him about my true condition, He could have used all that time to build my capacity, rather than to wake me up.

More doors open when we are honest. A friend who is a businessman was working on a partnership with a major manufacturer that had a very aggressive vision for their partnership. The vision, however, was beyond my friend's company's capacity to perform. He talked to me about it and found the simple solution: be honest! I said, "Tell them what you can do and what you cannot do and how you will build your capacity to handle the whole project."

My friend chose the honest route. Not everyone in business does. My friend's situation turned out well. The manufacturer agreed to his proposed scale-up.

We need to be truthful about who we are and where we are—with ourselves most of all.

> For I say, through the grace given to me, to everyone among you, not to think of himself more highly than he ought to think, but to think with sound judgment, according to the measure of faith God has distributed to every man.
> —ROMANS 12:3, MEV

We live in a society where projecting one's image is the norm. Social media has given everyone a platform, and many people believe their own press. We are like personal paparazzi and public relations people, taking and posting selfies and writing posts about how great we are. Too many of us have lost any sensible thinking about ourselves.

My brother-in-law is an executive for a major European company. One of his duties is to interview new employees. He says that most people have projected so much on their resumés that it is not worth looking at them. As applicants come in, he sets their resumés aside and engages them in a significant dialogue. He probes to see how they respond to questions they did not rehearse. He wants to get them to be honest.

This is the most important thing in our society. We need to be honest with honest people to do honest things in the name of an honest God.

Toward the end of His earthly assignment Jesus addressed the disciples who accompanied Him for three years. He informed them that many people would be offended because of Him. In Mark 14:29 Peter spoke boldly, as he often did: "Although all shall be offended, yet will not I" (KJV).

As we already saw, Jesus reminded Peter that the day to deny Him was at hand: "This day, even in this night, before the cock crow twice, thou shalt deny me thrice" (v. 30, KJV).

Peter still did not perceive his true position. The Bible says that he became vehement as he expressed his loyalty, saying, "If I should die with thee, I will not deny thee in any wise" (v. 31, KJV). Peter's convictions caused everyone else to make the same declaration. Now the whole group was projecting their loyalty to Jesus.

Isn't it odd that society uses the "honest to God" saying to lend credibility to their statements? The phrase is related to *honest-to-goodness* which is defined as "real or genuine"[3] People use God's name and His goodness to swear by. Why? Only God is good and God cannot lie. No one can be honest like God.

We are very skilled at deceiving ourselves, and after a while we can even begin to believe the falsehoods we have been telling others. Matthew's Gospel describes Peter standing outside the court where Jesus was being interrogated. One of the servants recognized Peter as one of Jesus's companions. Peter denied the association and said, "I do not know what you are saying" (Matt. 26:70).

This was the first denial that Jesus prophesied.

Someone else recognized Peter as a follower of Jesus. Peter refuted the accusation, saying, "I do not know the Man!" (v. 72). Peter was so caught up in saving his own life that he was willing to say anything. The text says that Peter made an oath. In essence he said, "I don't know the man, honest to God!"

To maintain the kind of internal resilience that could match the external pressure he faced, Peter's denials became increasingly aggressive. This is why "little lies" cannot stay little. Just when Peter thought he was in the clear, someone in the crowd provoked him yet again: "'Surely you also are one of them, for your speech betrays you.' Then [Peter] began to curse and swear, saying, 'I do not know the Man!' Immediately a rooster crowed" (vv. 73–74).

The level of intensity was too much. Peter lost all dignity and resorted to cursing, swearing, and lying. His state of mind soon deteriorated further: "Peter remembered the word of Jesus who had said to him, 'Before the rooster crows, you will deny Me three times.' So he went out and wept bitterly" (v. 75).

None of us like coming to terms with our real internal state, but before we can move to the next level, we have to repent for our current condition. Unless we realize who we really are, we cannot become who we want to be. We must be real with God, ourselves, and others. Honesty comes when repentance begins. Mercy comes when honesty begins.

Let's be honest, remembering that God is good and already knows and understands us. Jesus knew many months before that awful night that Peter lacked the strength to stand with Him in the courts of judgment or to die with Him on Calvary. It was not Peter's place to do that, but Peter refused to be honest with God.

Jesus wasn't shocked that Peter talked so big. He just kept telling Peter the truth. If Peter had accepted the truth early on, God could have told him how to respond to future events.

We can trust the Lord! He is merciful. Mercy is His display of power leading to restoration. God was merciful to Peter. Once the disciple was honest, God started working to restore him, through the words of a heavenly messenger:

> But he said to them, "Do not be alarmed. You seek Jesus of Nazareth, who was crucified. He is risen! He is not here. See the place where they laid Him. But go, tell His disciples—*and Peter*—that He is going before you into Galilee; there you will see Him, as He said to you.
>
> —MARK 16:6–7

I once heard Bill Wilson preach a message about times in our lives when we don't feel like we deserve God's love and mercy. Then God just goes the extra mile to reach us and love us.

Those who have made the worst mistakes need to be singled out with God's mercy and love. That is what He did for Peter when His messenger said, "But go, tell His disciples—and Peter." Why was Peter singled out? It was because Jesus knew that Peter would need more comfort at that moment than the other disciples did. Peter had fallen further than the others and only love could lift him up.

Love is God's plan to overcome condemnation. God is not a respecter of persons, but He knows what each of us needs to be restored. God is willing to give it, because He *is* love. Mercy in the time of dishonesty is a brilliant example of God's manifested love. It is what He did for Sarah when He renewed the promise, even though she lied to Him. He did the same for Peter. Though the man lied repeatedly and denied Jesus, God was looking to be good to him.

I realized a very important thing about God as I wrote this book: God will always be better than us! He would exhaust His resources to capture our hearts again. I know it is impossible for God to exhaust His resources, but if He could, He would do it for our sakes. Isn't that what He did when He sent His best—Jesus— to represent His goodness to us?

RESTORATION

The Bible says that Jesus knocks at the door and wants to come in and sup with us (Rev. 3:20). Something happens when people eat together. Boundaries are dropped and relationships are strengthened. Enemies won't eat together unless they are trying to make peace.

After His resurrection from the grave, Jesus showed Himself to His disciples again. The Bible says that He waited on the shore for them to return from a night of fishing. Jesus even had breakfast ready for them said, "Come and eat" (John 21:12).

After some time of fellowship, Jesus said to Peter, "Simon, son of Jonah, do you love Me more than these?" (v. 15).

Wow! What a probing question! Jesus was not looking for anything but an honest response. Peter said, "Yes, Lord; You know that I love You" (v. 15). This was the right answer.

Then Jesus asked Peter, "Do you love Me?" (v. 16), again using a word that indicates the kind of love that should only be given to God. Peter responded the same way as he had at first: "Yes, I love You but with a brotherly love" (vv. 15–16).

Peter's answer was honest, but he was still disappointed. He had failed his Lord before; now, he could not honestly profess the right kind of love for Him.

God is so good! Jesus honored Peter's honesty and understood his difficulty. So He asked one more time:

> "Simon, son of Jonah, do you love Me?" Peter was grieved because He said to him the third time, "Do you love Me?" And he said to Him, 'Lord, You know all things; You know that I love You."
>
> —JOHN 21:17

This time Jesus came down to Peter's level and asked whether Peter loved Him with a brotherly love. Peter's original sadness began with his dishonesty the night before Jesus died, but now Peter was grieved because Jesus lowered the standard to reach a place of honest agreement with His disciple. Peter would have to face his issues and repent of his disappointment.

Jesus was so merciful and did so much to restore Peter in this conversation. Remember that Peter denied Jesus three times. So Jesus gave Peter three opportunities to redeem himself by being honest. Jesus asked Peter to respond, not for His sake, but for Peter's. God often does this with us. He asks us to do things that restore us. They can never be classified as works; they are course corrections.

Jesus recalibrated and reinstated Peter by saying, "Follow Me" (v. 19). From the beginning this was all that Peter really wanted, but his disappointment and dishonesty held him back. Now he was free to follow his Lord—and he did!

Disappointment must be overcome before we can follow the Lord honestly. Be honest with Him and He will show you mercy and love. Never run; just be genuine.

Honesty is the best policy.

Part Three

LIVING IN GOD'S GOODNESS NOW

Chapter 14

I AM EXPECTING A VISITOR

When my wife expects a visitor, things get exciting around our house. She makes a shopping list of the person's favorite foods. We clean the house from top to bottom. We make plans to show our guest around the beautiful city of Seattle. Our goal is to be amazing hosts and to make visitors feel loved and comfortable.

Our family goes into expectation mode. But for that to happen, we must believe beyond a shadow of a doubt that our guest will show up. Otherwise we wouldn't expend all that energy preparing for their visit.

Just as our family's expectation is based upon our visitor's reliability, the believer's expectation is based upon God's reliability. Sarah found out how reliable He is:

> The LORD visited Sarah as He had said, and *the Lord did for Sarah as He had spoken.* For Sarah conceived and bore Abraham a son in his old age, at the set time that God had spoken to him. Abraham called the name

of his son who was born to him, whom Sarah bore to
him, Isaac.

—GENESIS 21:1–3, MEV

After much disappointment Sarah placed her faith in God's
faithfulness, then Isaac, a miracle and God's child of promise,
was born.

God is pleased by our faith in Him. Therefore it makes sense
that He would be faithful toward those who put their faith in
Him. Let me use another word instead of faith. God is pleased by
our *confidence.* Confidence touches God because He desires that
people would trust in His ability and His help. *Trust* is another
good substitute for the word *faith.* God is pleased by trust. He
wants us to know that He is completely trustworthy.

Whichever word we use, the point is that if we have no faith
in God, then we imply that something is wrong or lacking in
His character. It sounds self-evident, but those who lack faith
in God question His faithfulness. When they lack trust in God,
they question whether He is trustworthy. God doesn't just do
faithful and trustworthy things; faithful and trustworthy is
who He is! If He ever did something that was not either one,
He would be a liar.

Liars are untrustworthy, which sabotages their power to bond
with others. Trust, confidence, and faith are bonding agents.
They rest solely on the attribute of truth. If God lied, what would
hold the universe together? It is held together because He can
swear by His own ability that His words are good, always and
consistently. There is no greater name for God to swear by. Who
could possibly rise to the level of vouching for God's credibility?

You and I can confirm His faithfulness and trustworthiness
based on our belief and our experience. As we trust God, anyone
paying attention to our trust can see that He is in fact worthy
of it. As we live by faith, anyone paying attention to our faith in
God will see Him proven faithful. Our faith and trust in God
make Him visible to the world.

According to the following scripture, they also keep us in tune to the One who will not allow any temptation to overtake those who have faith in Him.

> No temptation has overtaken you that is not common to man. God is faithful, and he will not let you be tempted beyond your ability, but with the temptation he will also provide the way of escape, that you may be able to endure it.
> —1 CORINTHIANS 10:13, ESV

We can trust God to make a way of escape for us. Faith in God's faithfulness causes us to endure what we could never endure without Him. Faith in God's faithfulness is to believe beyond any circumstance that God is good and will do good on our behalf!

Our good God will make a way where there is no way and a way out of temptation—every time. Our faith in God's faithfulness drives us to hold on and not give up, long after everyone else has quit. It appears foolish to faithless people, but it is the supernatural reality that we live by.

When your soul, meaning your feelings and emotions, wants to give up, your spiritual mustard seed of faith is all you need to lock onto God's faithfulness and keep believing through the storms of life. Why? Because you know that God is faithful to His Word. He will do what He said He would do.

FAITHFUL TO HIS WORD

It is impossible to pull a credit report for God, but testimonials are a kind of report. The problem with testimonials is that God can be blamed for failing to do things He never promised to do in the first place. So God developed a simple system to prove that He is trustworthy. It is His Word, which He has obligated Himself to do. He didn't have to do it, but He wanted to show us His loving faithfulness.

What a powerful thought! God has thoroughly bound Himself to the promises in His creative words:

> I will worship toward Your holy temple and praise Your name for Your loving-kindness and for Your truth and faithfulness; for You have exalted above all else Your name and Your word and You have magnified Your word above all Your name!
> —PSALM 138:2, AMP

God's faithfulness is without end, and He has chosen to be intimately connected to us:

> God is faithful (reliable, trustworthy, and therefore ever true to His promise, and He can be depended on); by Him you were called into companionship and participation with His Son, Jesus Christ our Lord.
> —1 CORINTHIANS 1:9, AMP

Wow! God is faithful and true not only because He speaks the truth, but also because He is truth. Therefore whatever He says comes into existence. If something were not true before He said it, it would become true *because* He said it. If He declared that grass is blue, it would be blue from that moment on and no one could prove it was ever any different.

That should build your faith!

Everything conforms to God's Word because there is no truth outside of Him. God has no one greater than Himself to argue with and no one on His level who could call His words into question. Nothing is too big for God to handle. And because He is truth, everything that is true comes from Him.

Truth is a form of authority; because God *is* truth, He is the highest authority. His words create new truth in us. Second Corinthians 13:8 says: "For we cannot do anything against the truth, but only for the truth" (ESV). Much of the world believes that truth is relative, that it is developed and lived by individuals who determine its value. We can see from this verse that truth stands all by itself.

The Hebrew word *emet* (or *emeth*) means "faithfulness, truth."[1] In order to maintain faithfulness, we must maintain the truth. God's words are the only absolute truth. When God says, "I forgive your sins," His truth trumps any fact that described or governed your past. If God says that you are forgiven, it is true no matter how guilty you feel.

Two opposing systems stand before us continually: God's truth and our understanding of our experiences. Our faith in God's words must take precedence. Circumstances are fickle; they can cause us to feel rejected when they don't seem to go our way. When we lack solid faith and confidence in God, we get disappointed when things go wrong. We feel rejection, which is the root of disappointment.

When we begin to believe that God is good to us personally and would never leave nor forsake us, that belief will cause the root of rejection to be pulled up, removing both it and disappointment. We often look to the Word of God to learn why we have been disappointed; our time with God and His Word would be better spent discovering how good He really is.

The apostle John saw the divine goodness in the revelation he received:

> After that I saw heaven opened, and behold, a white horse [appeared]! The One Who was riding it is called Faithful (Trustworthy, Loyal, Incorruptible, Steady) and True, and He passes judgment and wages war in righteousness (holiness, justice, and uprightness).
>
> —REVELATION 19:11, AMP

Our God is good, faithful, and true. His name and Word set Him apart from any other authority. God is a Father who desires to do good things for His children. More than that, His name and Word are good. The authority of God's Word totally depends on His character.

God is faithful, therefore He is consistent. According to Jeremiah 29:11, God doesn't want us to be surprised by the end of our lives. He wants us to know exactly what He has planned. This knowledge enables us to recognize what is and what is not part of our destiny, so we know what to expect and what to reject.

Recently I ordered a salmon salad at a certain chain restaurant. It was delicious. A week later I went to the same restaurant in another city. This time the salad looked different. The lettuce was wilted. The salmon was colorless, refrigerator cold, and tasted like an aluminum can. I knew it was bad. If I hadn't known what to expect, I might not have known what to reject. God wants us to know what to expect; then we will confidently reject whatever is mediocre.

PERCEIVE AND TASTE

The worst thing we can do is to presume that we fully understand God's ways. We must continue to inquire of the Lord regarding every change in circumstance. When His heart becomes ours, we become faith-filled instead of doubtful. This is our way of escape.

The perfect example of this comes from Genesis 22 when Abraham and Isaac were on the mountain where Abraham expected to sacrifice his son. Abraham had carried out God's orders to the finest detail. He was prepared to sacrifice his son if he had to. Then a voice said: "Now that I know what's in your heart, don't kill your son." (See Genesis 22:12.)

Abraham obeyed, and God provided. Abraham saw a ram caught in the bushes; it was God's intended sacrifice. Now Abraham had more information about God's instruction and intent. God knew what was in Abraham's heart, and Abraham understood what was in God's heart.

More information will come once God knows what's in your heart. Do you trust in Him? Abraham did. He lived by faith and not sight, by perception and not presumption.

> Oh, taste and see that the LORD is good! Blessed is the man who takes refuge in him! Oh, fear the LORD, you his saints, for those who fear him have no lack! The young lions suffer want and hunger; but those who seek the LORD lack no good thing.
>
> —PSALM 34:8–10, ESV

In this passage *taste* is better translated "perceive," and *see* is better translated "experience." The insight behind the verses is that we as believers should not see and want. Our appetites should not be driven by what we see but what we believe. The appealing look of an apple should not prompt us to eat it. We should look at the apple and say, "God, You are amazing! It's wonderful how You have created this apple."

Your conversation with God about His creation should develop within you the desire to eat the apple. You want to eat it to prove what you perceive about God from His creation.

The act of perception is to taste intellectually, to first believe intellectually and without proof that the Lord is good, and then prove that He is good by partaking of what you have perceived. This gives glory to the Creator before you enjoy the creation. Everything that you partake of is a by-product of honoring Him.

Another thought about tasting and seeing that the Lord is good is the realization that you cannot eat the apple until you have blessed the Lord for it. According to Jewish law, eating the apple before thanking its Creator would be considered stealing. The Tehillim Hebrew commentary explains that if you see the apple and decide to bless God because of His amazing creation, you had to have made the decision beforehand that you would eat the apple. Think about it: if you see something with your spiritual eyes, you start thanking Him for it. God will then manifest it so you can experience it. Your faith in God will draw things from the world of the unseen into the seen realm. How does it work? Thank God for being good and watch the miraculous come to pass.

Tasting is spiritual and experiencing is natural, according to Psalm 34:8. Taste that God is good and experience the goodness of God. The passage does not stop with tasting and seeing, however. Psalm 34:10 explains that trusting our faithful and good God removes the curse of lack and want: "Those who seek the LORD lack no good thing." Disappointment comes from not seeing your desire come to pass, therefore it involves both lack and want. But the just don't live by what they see in the natural realm. They live by faith. Therefore disappointment is not for those who live by faith; it is only for those who live by sight.

Sarah is an amazing example of how to overcome an opportunity to be offended and disappointed. Ultimately her faith and hope superseded her disappointment. "By faith Sarah herself received power to conceive, even when she was past the age, since she considered him faithful who had promised" (Heb. 11:11, ESV).

Sarah maintained trust in the faithfulness of God, and it caused her to receive the power to conceive. Sarah *came back* from disappointment and was restored. Childbearing is the example in Sarah's life, but faith is the power to conceive any promise from God. Hope results from faith and acts as the midwife to help deliver the promise. Excitement is the epidural that helps the promise come more painlessly. Finally love is the very reason the promise is given in the first place.

God loved Sarah and was faithful, meaning He was steady in His allegiance and affection for her. Sarah found God to be both steady in allegiance and affection. She was past the age of childbearing, yet she conceived. Her body started doing things it had not done in years!

Imagine what Abraham experienced. Some men feel uncomfortable going to the store to buy feminine articles for their wives.

How about doing that when you are one hundred years old? God had to contradict in both their minds the facts of the natural realm. Sarah was naturally past fruitfulness, yet she was pregnant—she was *expecting.* The great expectation she would have known in her youth had come in her old age!

From conception, through faith, to hope, and to expecting—that's where Sarah was. That is how a promise is delivered. Faith conceives, hope believes, and patience receives.

Remember: expectation has an enemy. It speaks in the questions *what, why, how,* and *when.* These little words regulate some of the strongest emotions in life, especially when you are waiting for the fulfillment of your promise. Don't let them kill the momentum of your promise or detour your expectation. When you are tempted to ask, "What can I do to make things go faster? What should I expect? What is the problem?" just pause and remember to "taste and see that the Lord is good!"

SARAH'S VISITATION

Three visitors came to Abraham and Sarah's tent. It was a visitation from God, who came with certain details needed to restore Sarah's faith. Abraham's promise was entwined with Sarah's. He couldn't receive His promise until Sarah received hers. Abraham needed the visitation as much as she did.

A year later came another visitation; it was Sarah's visitation. "The LORD *visited Sarah* as he had said, and the LORD did to Sarah as he *had promised*" (Gen. 21:1, ESV). The Lord visited and did as He had promised. God has no problem tying Himself to a promise and bringing it to pass. He said the impossible thing would happen for Sarah and it did.

What can you count on God to do in your life? You can count on Him to do whatever He promises. Embrace through faith what God said and don't worry about what it will take to get it done. God's visitation is only associated with what He has promised. In the same manner His actions are only associated with what He has promised. In every case His promises are *yes* and *amen* (2 Cor. 1:20). They are as good as He himself is good.

Now let's study some elements of His promises.

The what

How do you find what God's promise is? By reading His book of promises—the Bible. You can confidently expect Him to do what is written in His book. The Word of God reveals the ways of God.

For example, He set up His promises for believers and has systematically set His angels to cooperate with the promises, as the psalmist explains: "Bless the LORD, O you his angels, you mighty ones who do his word, obeying the voice of his word! Bless the LORD, all his hosts, his ministers, who do his will!" (Ps. 103:20–21, ESV).

God's messengers obey God's voice, which is connected to His Word. As we believe it, understand His ways, and seek to do His will, we appropriate and activate His written promises, understanding His intent through the witness of the Holy Spirit.

The *what* can only be found in God's Word. Then you can discover the *why*.

The why

Why is a powerful word that gets to motivation. We ask questions such as, "Why did you do this?" "Why didn't you do this?" "Why isn't this working?" "Why should I push so hard?" "Why should I keep believing?" We ask why to understand what is behind the *what*.

Not every *why* question is looking for the right *why* answer. For example, why was Sarah so desperate to have a baby? We might imagine many reasons, but I believe Scripture reveals the answer: "Sarah conceived and bore *Abraham* a son in his old age at the time of which God had spoken to him" (Gen. 21:2).

Sarah bore *Abraham* a child. She was invested in being a part of fulfilling her husband's promise. Sarah's *why* was bigger than herself. It was wrapped up in her love for Abraham. It wasn't until God promised Sarah that she would be visited within twelve months that she had a promise of her own.

The only *why* worth fighting for must be based upon a dream bigger than yourself. Your dreams are intertwined with other people's promises. Your *why* is a necessary part of someone else's *why*. When your *why* is settled in your heart and mind, it will set you into action.

The power of *why* is behind every choice you make. *Why* functions in the limbic brain, the center of emotions. This affects goal setting, which is a necessary and powerful tool. The real power behind achieving your dream or pressing beyond your perceived limits is having a powerful and productive *why* that creates feelings and emotions compatible with the dream. Of course, anything you do in life must somehow be in response to God's goodness. If God hasn't given you a direct assignment, then get involved in someone else's dream, as Sarah did. Once God sees your commitment to fulfill another person's promise, He will in turn speak to you a promise that will unlock your own destiny.

Every promise must have the help and commitment of others to bring it to pass. Sarah's *why* was fulfilled in helping Abraham, which led to Sarah receiving God's miraculous power to conceive. In the process Sarah discovered that her faith was powerful too.

The how

How did Abraham and Sarah receive the promise? Scripture says this about Abraham:

> He did not weaken in faith when he considered his own body, which was as good as dead (since he was about a hundred years old), or when he considered the barrenness of Sarah's womb. No unbelief made him waver concerning the promise of God, *but he grew strong in his*

faith as he gave glory to God, fully *convinced* that God
was able to do what he had promised.
                                              —ROMANS 4:19–21, ESV

Abraham was fully convinced. Over many years he had developed faith in God's faithfulness. Sarah also gave glory to God in this regard. She saw His hand on her life when He rescued her from Abimelech by way of a dream (Gen. 20:3). Now although the opportunity for disappointment remained, both Abraham and Sarah had opportunity to recognize another level of God's love and faithfulness.

The *how* has a lot to do with outlasting the storm and trusting in a God whom you cannot see. How do you do that? How do you overcome disappointment and see your dreams come true? The answer is in your thinking, as Paul explained:

> Finally, brothers, whatever is true, whatever is honorable, whatever is just, whatever is pure, whatever is lovely, whatever is commendable, if there is any excellence, if there is anything worthy of praise, think about these things.
>   —PHILIPPIANS 4:8, ESV

We humans tend to think about whatever is bad. It seems to come naturally to us. Instead of taking inventory of all the good in our lives, we focus on what we believe is lacking. If we would continually take inventory of what is good, we would be more grateful and peaceful.

This is about how we keep our senses in check. Obviously Sarah and Abraham had taken presumptuous steps to fulfill the promise of God. That came from asking the wrong questions. Sarah's question was, "How is this going to come to pass?" Her answer was to find a younger, stronger body to stand in for her.

The questions we ask prepare us for either breakthrough or disappointment. Sarah might have asked, "How should I prepare myself for this?" or "What can I be thankful for today that will keep me focused on lovely things of a good report?" Had this been Sarah's approach, none of her suffering involving Hagar would have happened.

The *how* to receiving the promise is to quit asking the how questions that test God. Let God be God!

The when

"When?" is one of the most asked questions in history. The longer you and I wait, the greater the temptation to ask, "When?"

It happens on every road trip. Someone (usually a child) asks, "Are we there yet?" Adults have their more sophisticated way of asking: "When can we expect to arrive?" "When is it going to be my turn?" "When will I get married?" "When will I get the promotion?" "*When?*"

Just as children don't always understand how time and space work together, we don't always understand how God is working our circumstances for good. So we lose patience, often in a very short period of time. Would we be willing to wait for our promise as long as Abraham did? "Abraham was a hundred years old when his son Isaac was born to him" (Gen. 21:5, ESV).

The best advice I can offer for your *when* questions is this: simply walk in obedience to God's clear-cut instructions, while simultaneously looking for prophetic evidence that your hope is well placed. Avoid complaining and comparing; both are poison to the promise.

For Sarah to count God faithful and for Abraham to be convinced that He would reward their seeking, they had to avoid complaints and comparisons. These dysfunctional behaviors are from the devil himself. Without the knowledge of good and evil, there would be no complaining or comparison. Unfortunately society is built upon comparison. But that is not God's way.

There is a *when* that I would recommend. Know what you will do when the breakthrough finally comes. Sarah and Abraham were instructed to name their son *Isaac.* What a setup! *Isaac* means "laughter." The name is meaningful because names are very important in the Hebrew culture.

God prescribed Abraham and Sarah's response to Isaac's birth. We see it in the following verse:

> Abraham called the name of his son who was born to him, whom Sarah bore him, Isaac. And Abraham circumcised his son Isaac when he was eight days old, as God had commanded him.
> —GENESIS 21:3–4, ESV

First, Abraham named his son *Laughter,* which spoke of joy and stood as a reminder to laugh every day, on purpose! Then, by circumcising the promised child, he treated him as a gift that was sanctified and separated. And the separation of Isaac had to occur on the eighth day, signifying a new day and new beginnings.

When waiting for God's promise, we should laugh daily. We should determine that the promise we await is covenantal— a supernatural, sacred, and separated work of God. Finally we should expect that what God is doing is *new.*

EXPECTING AND PREPARING FOR VISITATION

"The Lord visited Sarah as he had said, and the LORD did to Sarah as he had promised" (Gen. 21:1, ESV). Sarah was told to look for her visitation, so she expected it.

We go about expecting a visitation the same way—by first of all knowing that it is coming. In Luke's Gospel the Lord warned His disciples about a missed visitation:

> For days will come upon you when your enemies will build an embankment around you, surround you and close you in on every side, and level you, and your children within you, to the ground; and they will not leave

in you one stone upon another, *because you did not know the time of your visitation.*
—LUKE 19:43–44

This tells us that unless we expect and prepare for the day of our visitation, *we can miss it.* God is all about preparation. The Bible says that God made preparation for us: "Oh, how abundant is your goodness, which you *have stored up* for those who fear you and *worked* for those who take refuge in you, in the sight of the children of mankind!" (Ps. 31:19, ESV). If God is prepared for us, shouldn't we also prepare for Him?

It is important to realize that God doesn't work spontaneously to meet our needs. He has planned in advance for us. As parents, my wife and I shop weekly to fill our pantry for our family. We make a list based upon what we need and would enjoy. We know that our kids like certain things. So we prepare for the day that they will want them. Our goal is to make provision available *before* our children need or ask for it.

We are God's children, and He is a good Father who knows exactly what we need and enjoy. Therefore He stores it up for us. He knew two years ago what you would need today. So He stored it up two years ago just for you. The truth is that He stored up all you will ever need and enjoy long ago, before the foundations of the world. It doesn't matter if you need it today, tomorrow, or fifty years from now. It's stored up for you. He is prepared!

I have had the privilege of ministering and speaking around the world. One specific occasion stands out regarding expectation and preparation. It was our first visit to South Korea. My wife and I were invited to speak at a minister's conference held at one of the many prayer mountains in the nation.

When we arrived, our host ushered us to our quarters—what looked like a brand-new apartment. We inquired about the room and were informed that the décor was in fact brand new. To prepare for our arrival they had completely gutted the apartment and installed new flooring, wallpaper, and furniture. They even filled the fridge with amazing fresh fruit.

They prepared just for us, working really hard to make us feel honored and loved. The previous furnishings would have been just fine. But they wanted us to feel special. They didn't do it for their own reward; they did it for our family.

God went to great lengths for Sarah too. He attended to every detail of His visitation. But she and Abraham also had to do their part. They had to prepare to be visited.

> The LORD *visited* Sarah as He had said, and *the Lord did* for Sarah as He had spoken. For Sarah conceived and bore Abraham a son in his old age, at the set time of which God had spoken to him.
> —GENESIS 21:1–2

Sarah conceived because the Lord visited her, but let's be real; there has been only one case of Immaculate Conception. So what happened to Sarah? Abraham and Sarah participated and prepared for the event.

Isaac's conception was supernatural but not immaculate. God *super* cooperated with Sarah and Abraham's natural activity to produce a supernatural conception. I am sure that Abraham and Sarah did not consider their participation to be "works." But it was the participation of expectation.

Preparation for a visitation is like holding out our hands ready to receive. This can only be done where expectation exists. Every so often my children come to me with their hands out, asking for money. I respond to the gesture and ask why they want the money. At the same time I reach into my pockets to see how much money I have.

My children are not trying to earn the money their hands wait for. That would be about works. *Work* is different from *works*. Works is the activity of earning what you desire. Work is preparation to receive what you desire. We cannot receive salvation from works, but we must work to prepare for a visitation.

We must have a work ethic to achieve our dreams. Athletes must work hard to prepare for their competitions. The Bible says we must work to enter into God's rest (Heb. 4:11). These things are done in preparation to receive. If we confuse *work* and *works,* all we will get is exhaustion.

Notice what Jesus invited us to do:

> Are you tired? Worn out? Burned out on religion? Come to me. Get away with me and you'll recover your life. I'll show you how to take a real rest. Walk with me and work with me—watch how I do it. Learn the unforced rhythms of grace. I won't lay anything heavy or ill-fitting on you. Keep company with me and you'll learn to live freely and lightly.
> —Matthew 11:28–30, The Message

Religion teaches that through our activity, God will approve us. But relationship with God says something else: He already accepts us and now we get to work with Him. We walk and work with the Lord through love and grace.

Paul the apostle explained to the church in Corinth how he was able to achieve great things by working with Christ: *"By the grace of God I am what I am, and His grace toward me was not in vain; but I labored more abundantly than they all, yet not I, but the grace of God which was with me"* (1 Cor. 15:10).

Paul described the perfect partnership between laboring and grace. When we expect God to do something, we prepare for God's grace to perform the heavy lifting. Paul achieved more than anyone else through the grace on his life.

A man named Zacchaeus learned about grace from Jesus. He also learned about visitation. Zacchaeus was a very rich tax collector. He heard that Jesus was coming to his town, so he went to where the crowd gathered, thinking, "Maybe I can just get a look at Him!" But Zacchaeus was short, "so he ran ahead and climbed up into a sycamore tree to see Him, for He was going to pass that way" (Luke 19:4).

Luke 19:3 specifically says that Zacchaeus was "of short stature." The word *stature* is used several times in the Bible to describe a person's development. Luke 2:52 speaks of Jesus growing in stature, meaning in "maturity."[2] Matthew 6:27 says that we cannot add to our stature by worrying.

Here's an interesting thought: perhaps worry stunts our spiritual and emotional intelligence. I realize that Zacchaeus was physically short. I also know the Bible never adds unnecessary details, but perhaps his height was not the real point.

Worry can keep us immature and emotionally stunted so that we can't see Jesus clearly. Some things in life don't mix well. Water and oil don't mix well. Faith and fear don't mix well. Worry and expectation don't mix well at all!

Zacchaeus's small stature is a spiritual metaphor. Spiritually speaking, he was a worrywart. His expectation in regard to seeing Jesus was the start of his overcoming previous limitations. It was so great that he wouldn't accept not being able to see past the crowd. He refused to be denied.

When you are fully persuaded and expecting, you won't take no for an answer. When you have a heightened sense of expectation, there is always a way. Possessed with expectation you will do the same two things Zacchaeus did. First, you will run ahead. That means thinking ahead and anticipating where the visitation will occur. The second thing you will do is find a higher vantage point.

We must think bigger than the obstacles. There will always be a crowd around your visitation. *Don't get distracted!* Get above the noise, above the hindrances, and above the rejection.

Zacchaeus ran ahead and climbed higher. His efforts paid off. When Jesus reached the place where Zacchaeus was, He looked up and saw him in the tree (Luke 19:5). Zacchaeus was not trying to get Jesus's attention. He was trying to see Jesus, so he prepared a place for himself.

The place he prepared so he could see Jesus became a place for Jesus to see him! The Bible says that when Jesus came to that place He looked up. Just a few minutes earlier that place wasn't a place at all. It wasn't until Zacchaeus went ahead and higher that it became a place.

Your expectation is also creating a place of visitation. Just seek to see the Lord, rather than seeking to get something from Him. Seeking to get something can be worry. Seeking Him first is expecting and trusting.

Jesus saw that Zacchaeus wasn't trying to make anything happen; he was only trying to see Him. Jesus called to the man in the tree saying, "'Zacchaeus, make haste and come down, for today *I must stay at your house.*' So he made haste and came down, and received Him joyfully" (v. 5).

Zacchaeus's preparations put a demand on Jesus. Jesus said, "I *must* stay at your house." Another way to say it is, "Your demand is causing Me to visit with you."

Our faith and hope in God moves Him to visit us. If we want Him more than we want anything else, He will give us the desires of our hearts. Zacchaeus's expectation caused him to receive more than just an opportunity to see Jesus. It created an opportunity for Zacchaeus to host the Messiah in his home!

Zacchaeus received the Lord joyfully. I imagine that his joy included smiling, leaping, clapping, and even laughing. It was a new beginning for Zacchaeus. By living in expectation, he positioned himself for a miracle.

Living in expectation will do the same for you!

Chapter 15

FULLNESS OF JOY

It was just as God promised. Within twelve months of God saying that Sarah would bear a child, she became strong enough to conceive and give birth! Sarah's source of strength is revealed in Hebrews 11:11: "By faith Sarah herself also received strength to conceive seed, and she bore a child when she was past the age, because she judged Him faithful who had promised."

It is evident that God strengthened Sarah to conceive. All Sarah could do was to put her faith in God's faithfulness. There are some very important life skills to be learned from this. First, Sarah's faith wasn't in herself but in God. And it wasn't all directed at having a baby; it was directed toward God. Nor was she trusting in her husband's faith. Sarah was past that place in her walk. Abraham had already discovered his faith and pleased God enough to be called righteous, but Sarah had to discover her own faith in God. Hebrews 11:11 shows that she did.

Something stands out to me: Sarah received strength to conceive seed. She then bore a son. She didn't receive strength to bear a son. Sarah received strength. Sarah didn't increase in strength; she received it. Nothing is impossible. Everything is possible with the proper strength. If we can gain the strength, we can do anything.

You can be just like Sarah, receiving the strength you need to do what you could not previously do. Strength is not something you earn or develop. Strength is being supplied to you. You simply need to receive it. Remember that holding out your hand causes the supplier to provide what is being requested. My kids hold out their hands, and I give them the money they need.

Once the supplier offers the help, the requester must receive the desired item. Sarah took the strength to conceive from the hand of a faithful God. *Received* in this case means "*to take... to take with the hand, lay hold of,* any person or thing in order to use it... to take up a thing to be carried, to take upon oneself."[1]

One time a friend of mine was in the mountains riding a snowmobile alone. He knew this was not a good idea from a safety perspective because if something happened there would be no one to help. And the worst-case scenario actually occurred: he had an accident, and the snowmobile crushed his thigh. He knew that his femur was broken and that he wouldn't be able to walk out or drive out. The only way off of the mountain was for God to intervene.

He prayed to his faithful God for healing, and instantly heat came over his leg so that he was able to get up and walk. God answered his prayer and gave him the strength to walk, retrieve his snowmobile, and get out. Just moments before, he was stranded and his femur was broken. After one prayer he was able to do what had been impossible. He received the strength to get himself off of the mountain.

That's what happened to Sarah. She was strengthened to conceive and then she bore. The strength of God was given and she received it. The Greek word used for strength in Hebrews 11:11 is the word *dunamis,* which is "strength, ability, power... inherent power, power residing in a thing by virtue of its nature, or which a person or thing exerts and puts forth...the power of performing miracles."[2]

Sarah was given the strength and power she needed because she judged that God was faithful. I was shocked to realize that the word *judged* here is completely different from what I understood the English word to mean. The Greek word is *hegeomai,* which means "to lead...to go before...to be a leader; to rule, command; to have authority over."[3] Sarah let God lead because He is faithful, true, and trustworthy.

We often believe that a promise allows *us* to lead. This could not be further from the truth. God needs to be the leader. He promised and therefore He knows how to get us to our destination. Remember that strength is received so that we can work alongside of God. God doesn't want to be unequally yoked, so He makes us strong enough to keep up with Him.

Because of their years in exile, the children of Israel were without the Torah. When they finally received the Word of God and realized how much space was between them and God, they began to weep from sorrow. Then Nehemiah and Ezra the priest told the people how they should respond to the Word:

> Go your way, eat the fat, drink the sweet, and send portions to those for whom nothing is prepared; for this day is holy to our Lord. Do not sorrow, for the joy of the LORD is your strength.
> —NEHEMIAH 8:10

Sorrow is not the proper response to God's amazing Word. The Bible is designed to bring us joy and give strength against sorrow and every form of oppression. Joy is God's syringe for injecting strength. That strength contradicts sorrow.

Both joy and sorrow are issues of the heart. Proverbs 4:23 says: "Keep your heart with all diligence, for out of it spring the issues of life." When you keep your heart, you can decide what flows from it. Whatever you allow to flow will determine the life you live. Check your heart continually. Don't only keep it, but also guard it with all diligence (guard it with a level of intensity).

Diligence means, "place of confinement...prison... guard, watch, observance...guard-house."[4] We are to guard our hearts as we would a prison, controlling what goes in and what goes out. So if you are the warden of your heart, you must lock sorrow in solitary confinement. Don't allow sorrow to see the light of day except on the rare occasions the Bible permits. For example, godly sorrow leads to repentance (2 Cor. 7:10). We are to sorrow with others, and we are to grieve reasonably when loved ones die (Rom. 12:15). Sorrow is never to be a lifestyle or lifelong commitment. Once sorrow has served its purpose, it must return to solitary confinement. Otherwise it is a destructive force finding opportunity to dictate our lives and torment us.

Joy can be trusted to run free. A life full of joy is a strong life. Joy in your family makes it strong. Joy in ministry or business makes them strong. The enemy understands this and tries everything possible to lock up your joy and let sorrow run free. Just as joy is associated with strength, sorrow is associated with weakness.

According to Proverbs 24:10, if we faint in the day of adversity, it's because our strength is small. Adversity should not exhaust our strength. If God is our source, we will have all the strength we need during adversity. Deuteronomy 33:25 says that "as your days, so shall your strength be."

Whatever kind of day that you are experiencing, you will have enough strength to keep from fainting. God's plan is to supply enough joy for you to handle every day, no matter what is transpiring. The joy flowing from your heart will result in a strong life.

Here is a scripture to build your faith in God's provision of joy: "You make known to me the path of life; in your presence there is fullness of joy; at your right hand are pleasures forevermore" (Ps. 16:11, ESV).

This tells me that God wants to make known to me the paths of life. There is a way that life should be walked out and God wants me to know exactly what that is. I can discover the issues of life and the paths of life only in one place: God's presence. That is where the fullness of joy is supplied. Every kind of joy possible is found there!

As believers we have access to God's presence at any given moment. Therefore we have access to the fullness of joy at all times. In God's presence there is a satisfaction of joy, fullness of joy, and every kind and level of delight. It is the answer for the disappointment we cannot shake, every fear that overwhelms, all anger that takes control, whatever sadness we cannot run from, and any hopelessness we feel unable to overcome.

Just run into His presence.

There are not words enough to express the power of joy we receive in the presence of the Lord. Each of us has to experience it for ourselves. If you have tried everything (medicine, vacation, distraction, etc.) and you cannot break through the dark cloud, find God in His presence and you will find the paths of life laden with complete and absolute joy.

There are many ways to enter into the presence of the Lord, but the key is sincerity. Approach Him with a sincere heart and you will find Him. Worship in song, prayer, and through scripture will lead you to a loving and kind God and all the strength and joy you need for the journey.

OVERCOMING SORROW

Emotions don't lead; they follow. God has a time for everything. We should limit how long our emotions run in specific directions, just as God does: "His anger is but for a moment, His favor is for life; weeping may endure for a night, but joy comes in the morning" (Ps. 30:5).

Anger is not supposed to be a way of life, but the experience of favor is. Weeping is short-lived and shouldn't be given place for more than a night, but joy should be new every morning. If sorrow brings you to tears, consider those moments to be times of sowing, with each tear a seed that will be harvested as joy (Ps. 126:5).

Jesus has secured a lifelong transaction guaranteeing that our sorrow will always be turned to joy. Before His death on the cross, He told His disciples: "Most assuredly, I say to you that you will weep and lament, but the world will rejoice; and you will be sorrowful, but your sorrow will be turned into joy" (John 16:20).

Jesus has turned every sorrow we would ever experience into joy—not just an earthly and carnal joy, but His own joy given to us.

JOY FROM WHAT HE SAYS

In John 15:11 we are to receive what He says: "These things I have spoken to you, that My joy may remain in you, and that your joy may be full." What Jesus speaks to us causes His joy to fill our joy tank and keep it full. Christ's joy is more than enough. It abides in us and is available every morning and in every moment. His joy is a receiver for our joy.

This seems to be God's mind toward us. He wants His joy to be on tap for us. Look at John 16:24: "Until now you have asked nothing in My name. Ask, and you will receive, that your joy may be full." We clearly see that God reserves joy so we can tap in anytime we need it. In this case it comes from asking and receiving—not just asking for joy, but asking for and receiving whatever is needed. Jesus encouraged us to expect our prayers to be answered and received with unhindered joy.

I believe it is important for us to fully associate the Word with joy. God wants us to be joy-full. We are to be filled up, abounding, furnished, and supplied liberally with joy that never runs out. We never saw Jesus run out of joy, so neither should we. And if we do, we can tap in to His reservoir and make our joy full again.

Joy in shouts of victory

When the children of Israel received the ark of God back into their camp, they shouted so loudly from joy that it scared the Philistines, who wondered, "What does this great shout mean?" The shout of joy unnerved the Philistine army (1 Sam. 4:5–8). I believe that a shout of joy still unnerves the enemy because it is a posture of victory—even a victory that is not yet seen.

The Philistines didn't understand why the children of Israel were shouting this way; they hadn't won the war yet. The Israelites were shouting because they had the presence of God back with them. They lost that war because they didn't fully embrace God's words, but they received joy from His presence. From there they could reach the next level: to receive strength to overcome the enemy.

After thirty-eight years our football team, the Seattle Seahawks, won their first Super Bowl. The "12th man" (aka, the Seahawks fans) had been growing more and more radical each year, even though the Seahawks had never won a Super Bowl. Seahawks fans have been known to be the loudest in the world, constantly pushing the decibel level to support their team and give them the winning edge.

A few weeks before the 2013 Super Bowl, the 12th man broke another record. They created such a level of joy and excitement in the stadium that it registered an earthquake. If football fans can move the ground with natural joy, what can we move with joyful shouts of victory in our homes, schools, or cities?

David understood shouts of joy and wrote about them in Psalm 27:6: "Now my head shall be lifted up above my enemies all around me, and I will offer in his tent sacrifices with shouts of joy; I will sing and make melody to the LORD" (ESV).

When an enemy is near, we shouldn't be silent. We should be in the pavilion of God, sacrificing shouts of joy not fear. That is where victory comes from, but the idea is counterintuitive. Some would ask, "Who in their right mind would take time to gather a sacrifice and offer it to the Lord, instead of preparing for the battle?"

A king did it! King David learned the art reigning in the midst of his enemies. Instead of running to battle, he chose to run to his King and sacrifice on His altar with shouts of joy. David prepared for battle by approaching God with the understanding that God would lift his head above his enemies. He believed that God would give him the wisdom, strategies, authority, governmental abilities, and superior anointing his enemies could not muster.

David trusted God to do all this. He had learned the power of joy early on. When his best men were ready to stone him, David encouraged himself in the Lord (1 Sam. 30:6).

We too must learn the art of joyful singing and shouting. Scripture tells us to "Let the word of Christ dwell in you richly, teaching and admonishing one another in all wisdom, singing psalms and hymns and spiritual songs, with thankfulness in your hearts to God" (Col. 3:16, ESV). In Ephesians 5:19 we are again challenged to address "one another in psalms and hymns and spiritual songs, singing and making melody to the Lord with all your heart" (ESV).

Every week in Sunday schools around the world children and grownups are learning that God is in their hearts. If we believe that, we need to act as if He's in us and sacrifice shouts of joy and praise from and to our hearts. In other words, we allow the joy to come from the Lord within us, and we also send our shouts of joy to Him who is in our hearts. It's sad to see believers in Christ turning on themselves in difficult times. They talk to and about themselves as though the Lord does not live in them. Many speak in ways that they would never speak to the Lord. Yet when they talk to themselves, they *are* talking to the Lord who is in their hearts.

When David encouraged himself in the Lord, he "*chazaq Yĕhovah elohiym*," which literally translated means he "strengthened the existing One ruler and judge," according to Strong's concordance. So in fact, David encouraged God! When we are in the battle, we need to shout joy and victory to God as our champion who is going to come from the shadows to secure the victory. He is our secret weapon!

King David went into the tents of sacrifice and shouted joyfully. As King David sacrificed he *tĕruw`ah,* which is a shout of joy. But the meaning of the word is far more than simple joy. King David made a "signal, sound of tempest, shout or blast of war or alarm or joy, alarm of war, war-cry, battle-cry, blast (for march), shout of joy (with religious impulse)."[5] King David's shouts of joy were a battle cry for God to arise and let all of His enemies be scattered (Ps. 68:1).

Before King David could courageously say, "I would have fainted if I didn't believe to see the goodness of the Lord in the land of the living." (See Psalm 27:13.) He first needed to get God's attention through joyful shouts. King David preceded war with joy, but he also celebrated the victory in joy:

> They pushed hard to make me fall, but the LORD helped me. The LORD is my strength and my song. He is my savior. The sound of joyful singing and victory is heard in the tents of righteous people. The right hand of the LORD displays strength.
> —PSALM 118:13–15, GW

God's strength was displayed as King David displayed joy. Our duty is to celebrate God joyfully before and after the battle. Then His response will be to win the battle through His strength.

Weapons for joy

Joel chapter 3 is full of insight on how to position ourselves in war. This is what needs to happen to overcome sorrow and move into a life of joy. Though the result seems carefree, the pursuit is warlike. We learn that everyday items can be transformed into weapons of war if we apply them with purpose and force.

Joel 3:10 says: "Beat your plowshares into swords and your pruning hooks into spears." Elsewhere Scripture is clear that swords and even spears (which are basically extended swords), are the Word of God (Eph. 6:17). We must let our everyday words become weapons of war by changing them from things used to sow and reap into instruments of battle.

The passage from Joel continues and raises the bar by stating the objective of our words. It says: "Let the weak say, 'I am strong'" (Joel 3:10). We should use our words to attack weakness and build strength. Our words are forceful; they can keep us weak or make us strong.

Joel 3 continues and takes us in another direction, building a picture of making good choices. It returns our thoughts to a previous battle, saying: "Let the nations be wakened, and come up to the Valley of Jehoshaphat; for there I will sit to judge all the surrounding nations" (v. 12).

In the battle of Jehoshaphat the nation was awakened to a new form of battle—worship (2 Chron. 20). The Lord told Israel that the battle was His and He promised that He would fight for them. He was asking them to trust Him on a whole new level: King Jehoshaphat led the nation into a battle weaponized only with praise and worship.

The Valley of Jehoshaphat is a place where you must decide to trust God enough to arm yourself with only worship. This is where you learn to let God fight your battles on your behalf. He will destroy the works of the devil in your life as you shout for joy. It might take more than one shout. Just don't stop! Let many shouts of joy resound from the tents of those who belong to God! The battle is not yours. It might feel like it is up to you, but it is not. It is up to God to give the victory.

Choose life and victory! Shout!

Chapter 16

GOD MADE
ME LAUGH

When three visitors came with good news for Sarah, she laughed. It's no wonder. She had suffered decades of disappointment and was told that she would give birth when her body was incapable of doing any such thing.

Sarah would laugh in the end and be freed from disappointment. She would hold her son, whose literal name was *Laughter*, knowing that it was only by God's grace and power that he had been conceived.

> And the LORD visited Sarah as He had said, and the LORD did for Sarah as He had spoken. For Sarah conceived and bore Abraham a son in his old age, at the set time of which God had spoken to him. And Abraham called the name of his son who was born to him—whom Sarah bore to him—Isaac. Then Abraham circumcised his son Isaac when he was eight days old, as God had commanded him. Now Abraham was one hundred years old when his son

Isaac was born to him. And Sarah said, "God has made
me laugh, and all who hear will laugh with me."
                                    —GENESIS 21:1–6

Joy and laughter are dynamic weapons. We have seen in the
Scriptures how God chose laughter to be a weapon of war. Psalm
2:4 provides a glimpse: "He who sits in the heavens shall laugh;
the Lord shall hold them in derision." We also see the Lord
laughing in Psalm 59:8 and in Psalm 37:13. He is so into laughing
at the enemy that He raised us up into heavenly places (see Eph.
2:6). Now we can sit in heaven and laugh along with Him.

We make it very clear to everyone who joins our ministry
team that laughter is a necessity. They need to understand this
part of our culture before they come onboard. We deal with
serious issues every day. We don't need to be stiff and stoic. If we
cannot laugh on purpose, we will surely burn out or break down.

I love what Sarah says: "God has made me laugh" (Gen. 21:6).
Let me ask you a question: When was the last time God made
you laugh? Laughter is a God emotion. He is funny! He has a
better sense of humor than any person who has ever lived. We
need to understand God's sense of humor. He loves to make us
laugh through His goodness.

Religious and traditional thinking have tried to convince us
that laughter is unholy. Maybe that is because "religious" people's laughter is still associated with unholy and profane images
and thoughts. I know that when we walk into heaven we will
hear pure, uncontrollable laughter and joy.

Rabbinic commentary teaches that Sarah's joy became contagious, a miracle for everyone in the community. It also states
that when Sarah gave birth to Isaac, many in the community
were healed. I believe God wants to do the same with you and
me. He wants to give us miracles that affect whole communities.
Our freedom will make other people free!

Mark Twain said, "Before the assault of laughter nothing can
stand."[1] I like the idea that laughter is an assault weapon able to

defeat horrifying enemies. Some scientists agree with the idea; I have incorporated into this chapter snippets from articles that show how potent laughter is as a medicine and weapon of war. We must realize that the Bible is the truth, and science works very hard to know and understand the truth. Proverbs 17:22 describes the healing virtues of laughter saying: "A joyful heart is good medicine, but a crushed spirit dries up the bones" (ESV).

Science agrees that laughter reduces stress hormones, lowers blood pressure, and reduces the risk of heart attack and stroke. Laughing improves your immune system by generating more disease-fighting cells.[2]

Lee Berk, a preventive care specialist and psychoneuroimmunologist from Loma Linda University, studied the effects of laughter on diabetes patients. Berk and his colleagues divided twenty diabetics into two groups: Group C (control) and Group L (laughter). The researchers treated members of both groups with common medications and tested their blood for stress hormones regularly for twelve months. Group L was also given thirty minutes to view humorous videos of their choice.[3]

This therapy was implemented for one year. After two months all patients in Group L had lower epinephrine and norepinephrine, which is believed to cause stress. Testing also revealed lower levels of inflammation. After twelve months good cholesterol increased 26 percent in Group L but only 3 percent in Group C.[4]

The group that watched comedy increased in some measure of immune function such as T-cell activity (important to handling infection), natural cells killer (which works against tumor growth), and other benefits.[5]

Laughter stimulates your mind, emotions, and body to release a variety of "feel good" chemicals from endorphins to dopamine and oxytocin. Laughter also helps to flush out toxins as it gets your lungs working and your heart pumping more effectively. One minute of rigorous laughter has been shown to produce many of the same cardiovascular benefits as ten minutes on a rowing machine and fifteen minutes on a stationary bike! You can even burn calories simply by laughing![6]

I have seen the healing power of laughter firsthand. A friend of mine was diagnosed with a rare cancer in her organs. She came to a healing service at our church. We had special guests, Georgian and Winnie Banov, in service with us that night. Winnie and I felt the direction of the Lord to laugh over the woman with cancer.

Yes! Laugh!

Although God is the same yesterday, today, and forever; He doesn't always do things the same way. The woman went to the doctor and found that she had been *completely* healed of cancer.

Laughter is contagious because it is not only emotionally centered, but it is also physical and mechanical. Laughter works in our brains, in the hypothalamus. Researchers have discovered: "Laughter also creates a high-frequency energetic state, which many refer to as 'bliss.' While in this state, your body literally tingles with joy! In fact, laughter has been equated with the full activation of the brain's left frontal lobe or 'jolly center,' which also happens to coincide with enlightenment."[7]

Sorrow deactivates the jolly center and enlightening process. This hinders our problem solving and innovation capacities during trials and only prolongs the problem. The best response to a problem is to laugh about it and activate your jolly creativity!

BRAIN WORKS

Humor and laughter affect the brain, which affects the emotions. This is because the limbic system is involved in all emotions, including laughter.

Most of us know laughter can be contagious. Steven Small, a professor in neurology and psychology, argues that the contagious nature of laughter is due to "mirror neurons" or "brain cells that become active when an organism is watching an expression or behavior that they themselves can perform."[8]

When you see someone laughing, you can begin laughing, even if you don't know what the laughter is about. Laughter is an effective stress-management tool because it lowers the level of stress hormones while increasing the release of the body's natural painkillers (endorphins).

Science is still stumped about the origin of laughter. Of course, it is known that some people laugh because they are nervous. Others laugh at things and situations that seem odd to the rest of us. Some get the jokes so late they shouldn't be laughed at anymore, yet even late laughter gets a laugh from those who find humor in the delay.

According to psychotherapist Enda Junkins, who specializes in laughter therapy: "In order to achieve laughter one combines play with serious issues. Play may incorporate a different way of thinking, word play, props, phraseology, etc. Playfulness is not synonymous with silliness so one need not fear losing one's adult dignity. Interestingly laughter alone will not suffice to completely deal with issues. As feelings are accessed, crying, anger, work, and talking are often necessary along with laughter. Emotions are held in the body and all means of catharsis are necessary to heal. Which ones and how much depend on the individual. Laughter is perhaps the most important because it releases three emotions (anger, anxiety and boredom) and it is the most pleasant and often the most acceptable."[9]

Cancer research centers use something called laughter therapy to bring healing. It's being used to treat many physical and emotional ailments. People watch funny programming, tell and listen to funny stories, and experience belly laughs to be healed.[10]

If the power of natural laughter can release healing, how much more can laughing out loud at the goodness of God bring freedom? People resist laughter because they think that it's just an emotional response, but laughter involves your spirit, soul, and body.

198 THE ART OF JOY

Laughter is a sign that a person's heart is joyful. Joy is good medicine. Disappointment is a sign that a person's heart is full of sorrow. Proverbs 17:22 shows the ugly side of a sorrowful heart: "a crushed spirit dries up the bones." Dried bones are a literal side effect of disappointment. Just as laughter's side effects are spiritual, emotional, and physical, so are the effects of disappointment. It destroys our ability to resist opposition and push into the next level. It causes us to quit easily and early. It may even prevent us from trying. Disappointment leaves its victims vulnerable and feeling victimized.

Why aren't you laughing? Is it because you see laughter as only a reaction to a stimulus? Do you hear yourself saying, "Something or someone will finally make me happy. Someone needs to make me laugh. Let me call So-and-So because I need a good laugh"? When was the last time you laughed out loud by yourself? At yourself? On purpose? Try it! Laugh out loud right now…go ahead!

Some of you started laughing at the thought. Others considered what other people would think. And some of you wouldn't even try. You just kept on reading.

Why aren't you laughing? What is the first thing that breaks down in a relationship? Laughter. It's because laughter is connected to the heart. Let your heart laugh. Tell your mind to be quiet and just open your mouth and start laughing.

Go ahead! Laugh!

If you tried it, you probably started off by faking it. Then something in your heart kicked in and took over. The truth is that we only laugh at what we have already decided is funny and only with those whom we trust. Most people don't think they are funny, and they don't trust themselves. Of course, if you think that God is funny, you will find more things that He finds funny than sad ones. If you trust God, you will laugh much more easily.

Let your heart take courage. Reevaluate what makes you laugh. Decide that laughing out loud on purpose is good, not weird. Develop your laughing muscles to the point that you can laugh at any moment, regardless of the circumstance.

That sounds ridiculous doesn't it? But it's necessary. Why aren't you laughing? Maybe it's because you take things too seriously. Maybe you have been disappointed one too many times. Maybe it's because you're too busy to take in each and every moment. If you and I can be delivered from ourselves, then maybe we can enjoy life.

Listen: the devil didn't find a place (a hook) in Jesus because Jesus emptied Himself of all reputation. He had no ego, pride, arrogance, shame, guilt, or self-seriousness that the devil could latch on to.

When Satan can't find a hook in you and me, then we can laugh when he tries to intimidate us. Satan hates to be laughed at, because he's loaded with pride. You should laugh in his face right now, on purpose. He loves fear, seriousness, stoicism, anger, and pride, but he can't handle rejoicing. Laughing on purpose at the goodness of the Lord is the ultimate weapon of warfare against Him.

Praise and worship leads us to the feet of God. We should find ourselves in a puddle of joy, melting from the goodness that is found in His presence. Laughter is part of our praise, worship, and thanksgiving!

> When the LORD restored the fortunes of Zion, we were like those who dream. Then our mouth was filled with laughter, and our tongue with shouts of joy; then they said among the nations, "The LORD has done great things for them." The LORD has done great things for us; we are glad.
> —PSALM 126:1–3, ESV

God wants to be the center of our laughter and joy. He wants us to laugh for joy over promises, before and after they are fulfilled. God desires to hear His children laughing. He made the children of Israel feel as if they were in a dream, as if life was too good to be true. When favor and fortune are restored to you, it's supposed to make you feel as if you are in a dream. It's supposed to feel as if it's too good to be true.

If you have experienced loss, it's not from God. God wants to restore you to laughter and joy. He desires to restore everything so that He can fill your mouth with laughter and your tongue with shouts of joy. The Lord will show His greatness by making you glad.

THE FIRST LAUGH

Where does laughter come from? Finding the first mention of a topic in the Bible gives us greater understanding of the subject. Laughter is both mentioned first and mentioned most in connection to the story of Isaac's birth.

We must look deeper into Scripture for insight from God. Keep in mind that Abraham and Sarah spent thirteen years raising Ishmael as their heir to the blessing. God was silent during those years. After thirteen years He finally reopened the conversation with Abraham. He reassured Abraham that He was not mad at him, but He opened a can of worms:

> God said to Abraham, "As for Sarai your wife, you shall not call her name Sarai, but Sarah shall be her name. *I will bless her,* and moreover, I will give you *a son by her.* I will bless her, and *she shall become nations;* kings of peoples shall come from her. Then *Abraham fell on his face and laughed* and said to himself, "Shall a child be born to a man who is a hundred years old? Shall Sarah, who is ninety years old, bear a child?"
> —GENESIS 17:15–17, ESV

God brought clarity that He had not given Abraham and Sarah when the promise was first mentioned. He renamed Abram *Abraham,* and here changed Sarai's name to Sarah. The reason goes beyond definitions. The letters themselves had significance. In Hebrew each letter has a meaningful numerical value. God removed the "i" from Sarai. The letter has a numerical value of "ten." God split the number ten or the letter "i" into two fives. The alphabetical meaning of five is "h." God gave one "h" to Abraham (when He changed his name from Abram). God gave the other five back to Sarai, now *Sarah*.

This represented that the future of Abraham was to come through Sarah. Sarai was to go from a princess, to Sarah, a noble woman—a queen.

God's conversation made it clear to Abraham that Sarah would bring about the heir. He said, *"I will bless her,* and moreover, I will give you a son *by her.* I will *bless her,* and *she shall become nations;* kings of peoples shall come *from her."* If Abraham was ever unsure about who would carry the promised child, he could no longer have any doubt.

Sarah heard directly from God about how much He believed in her. Before that day Sarah didn't know that she was going to become a nation; she had no idea that kings were inside of her.

You may not know what is inside of you, but there is still more to come out of you. God put something inside of you at the foundations of the world that hasn't been revealed yet. Don't give up now. There is a king or queen inside of you. There is nobility inside of you.

God's conversation with Abraham was so amazing that it caused him to fall to his face and laugh at how good God is and desired to be. Abraham *tsachaq,* meaning he laughed outright. This is the first laugh mentioned in the Bible. It's a laugh inspired by the goodness of the Lord.

THE SECOND LAUGH

The second laugh is recorded when Sarah overheard the conversation between God and Abraham when the three visitors came:

> So *Sarah laughed to herself,* saying, "After I am worn
> out, and my lord is old, shall I have pleasure?" The LORD
> said to Abraham, "Why did Sarah laugh and say, 'Shall I
> indeed bear a child, now that I am old?'"
> —GENESIS 18:12–13, ESV

Rabbinical commentaries tell us that both Abraham and
Sarah laughed from sheer joy. The Hebrew word *tsachaq* means
"to laugh." Rabbi Daniel Lapin writes about the *tsachaq* in his
book *Buried Treasure:* "In regard to the birth of Isaac, Sarah
laughs in joy at the miraculous event of an old lady giving birth.
There is something here that defies the expected course of event."
Rabbi Lapin goes on to write: "Most laughter we hear each day
is in response to this general pattern."[11] Laughter is one way of
responding to something that conflicts with our expectation.
Both Abraham and Sarah laughed, but they laughed for different reasons. Abraham didn't laugh to himself or at himself.
He laughed outright and then said something to himself. Sarah
laughed to herself, while saying something about herself.

Our patriarch and matriarch had reconciled themselves
to Ishmael being the heir. Abraham laughed not because an
Isaac seemed impossible, just more complicated. Sarah laughed
because the idea of having a child was a lost memory and desire.
Her response, "After I am worn out, and my lord is old, shall I
have pleasure?" (Gen. 18:12, ESV). She was already past this option.

Both Abraham and Sarah were old but only one of them
had lost the natural ability for childbearing. The Scripture says:
"Now Abraham and Sarah were old, advanced in years. The way
of women had ceased to be with Sarah" (Gen. 18:11, ESV). If we
don't trust in our natural ability, we are left with trusting only in
God's ability.

Sarah was a spiritual woman, but she doubted her own ability
to carry out God's goodness. When we worry about what, how,
and when the promise may come to pass, we are drawn into the
natural—no matter how spiritual we may be. When we seek first

the kingdom of God and His righteousness, we become more lighthearted and free from worry. Worry kills laughter, unless we make the Lord our shepherd and allow Him to set us free from want and worry!

Disappointment causes us to laugh when God's goodness seems unlikely to us, but as we continue to think about His words, we begin to feel hope again. When Sarah laughed, God asked Abraham point-blank: "Why did Sarah laugh and say, 'Shall I indeed bear a child, now that I am old?'" (Gen. 18:13, ESV).

God locked in on the real issue: the part about being too old. Sarah was focused on her ability to be used, rather than on God's desire to use her.

Here is a word for all of us: don't allow your feelings from the past to stop what God is trying to do for you today!

God settled the issue with Sarah when He asked: "Is anything too hard for the LORD? At the appointed time I will return to you, about this time next year, and Sarah shall have a son" (Gen. 18:14, ESV). He hit the voice of disappointment head-on. We need to do the same when the odds are against us. We should ask: "Is anything too hard for the Lord?"

Sarah was hung up on her history. She knew where she was physically. She'd never known anyone who gave birth at her age. She tried her own workaround, and it was a disaster. Then God gave her a visual picture of what the promise looked like and time-stamped it. It was still hard for Sarah to imagine, but it was not her job to comprehend.

It is our duty to believe *before* we comprehend.

Experiences and circumstances are always the tools used to steal our hope in God. If we would believe in God in the midst of unfortunate circumstances and undesirable life experiences, we would know what real believing is.

God set up Sarah so she could rise to a new level of faith in Him. He asked her to believe in Him in a way that He had never asked anyone before. It would be enough to make anyone laugh!

THE THIRD AND FOURTH LAUGHS

The third laugh was when Sarah gave birth to Isaac. The third laugh caused many people to laugh with her. "Sarah said, "God has made me laugh, and all who hear will laugh with me" (Gen. 21:6).

It's important to note that the first three laughs recorded in the Word of God had to do with the goodness of the Lord. It is very important that we find ourselves laughing with God, not at things that He wouldn't have anything to do with. The enemy has worked viciously to take over humor to use it in perverted ways, such as ridicule. Ridicule is meant for judgment against the enemy. It is not for the children of God.

Laughter is also designed by God to be the shortest distance between two people. People who laugh together grow together. God wants us to build relationships around what we laugh over together.

The fourth laugh was of the dark variety, not building unity, but pitting brother against brother:

> So the child grew and was weaned. And Abraham made a great feast on the same day that Isaac was weaned. And Sarah saw the son of Hagar the Egyptian, whom she had borne to Abraham, *scoffing.* Therefore she said to Abraham, "Cast out this bondwoman and her son; for the son of this bondwoman shall not be heir with my son, namely with Isaac."
>
> —GENESIS 21:8–10

On the very day that Isaac moved into manhood, Abraham put on a feast. At the feast Sarah saw the son of Hagar the Egyptian scoffing. Scoffing is the same word *tsachaq.* I find it interesting that the Bible didn't use Ishmael's name in this circumstance. What Ishmael was doing was not a part of Abraham's culture. The Bible draws a clear cultural distinction through its choice of words: "Sarah saw the *son of Hagar the Egyptian,* whom she had borne to Abraham, scoffing" (Gen. 21:9). Ishmael was acting like an Egyptian rather than a Hebrew.

Jewish commentary on verse 9 are as follows: "Mocking [or: playing; making sport]. This term expresses what Sarah saw that convinced her that Ishmael could not remain in the household. Scripture uses this verb to denote the three cardinal sins: idolatry [Exodus 32:6]; adultery [(Genesis) 39:17]; and murder [II Samuel 2:14]. Thus Ishmael's behavior proved that he had become thoroughly corrupt and evil, and he had to be sent away (*Rashi*)."[12] These three cardinal rules were given to Abraham: no idolatry, adultery, or murder; but Ishmael wasn't acting like his father. Obviously Hagar didn't fully embrace Abraham's rules. Ishmael learned his humor from Hagar's side of the family. If your son is named Isaac, "laughter," you would want to make some rules around the house about laughing.

The world's rules about humor are these: the more sexually oriented, violent, racial, and anti-religious it is, the funnier it is. Ishmael's behavior was improper and would have corrupted Isaac if he were allowed to stay. I believe that Ishmael was jealous of Isaac. When Ishmael was thirteen, God interrupted Abraham just before He could make Ishmael the heir of the blessing. Now that Isaac was becoming a man, Ishmael saw something between Isaac and his father that Ishmael and his father never shared. Ishmael revealed his lack of dignity and character at this point, when he purposefully tried to corrupt the new heir of the blessing.

Much of the world's strategy of humor is still based upon the violation of the three cardinal sins: religion, sex, and violence. Evil and wicked people find these things humorous. Remember the warning not to sit in the seat of the scorner (Ps. 1:1). The righteous will not sit in on a comedian whose humor is ungodly.

The laugh of Abraham at the goodness of God was a spiritual laughter response. Sarah's laughter in response to hearing the goodness of the Lord was a natural response. Ishmael's laugh came from a wicked heart that delighted in breaking God's cardinal rules. The Word of God carefully revealed all three types of laughter for a reason.

So what's the point? Not all laughter is created equal. There are many types of laughs; the snort, the honk, snicker, and howl. The list goes on! But we must also take into account that laughter comes from the heart, and anything that proceeds from the heart is in essence spiritual. There are three main natures of laughter, just as there are three natures to man: spiritual, social, and physical. Spiritual things always affect our spirits, souls, and bodies. We must live, laugh, and love with all of our being (Deut. 6:5, Mark 12:30, 1 Thess. 5:23).

BECOME LIKE LITTLE CHILDREN

Matthew 18:3 says: "Assuredly, I say to you, unless you are converted and become as little children, you will by no means enter the kingdom of heaven."

Statistics reveal how many more times a child laughs in a day than an adult does. It is said that a child laughs three hundred to four hundred times each day, but an adult laughs only ten to fifteen times. Whether or not this is true, I am sure that children laugh much more than adults. Why? Adults use their brains to first understand the humor and then they laugh. Many call this the Mind-to-Body Model or the Humor Model. The children's model is the Body-to-Mind Model. Their laughter bypasses their intellect and comes from laughter's starting place: the body.[13]

You can tap into this source at will. You can stimulate laughter just by moving your body and acting childlike. When people are happy, they are more energetic and expressive. When people are sad, they move less and are dull and unemotional. Allow the Lord to make you laugh. Treat joy and laughter as a form of worship and spiritual warfare. When you laugh with God, you are disobedient to the five natural senses—and that's a good thing.

There is a lady in my church whom we will call Susan. Susan came to us after eighteen years of depression. Her husband had abandoned her, leaving her devastated. Eventually Susan stopped going to church and spent much of her life in bed.

One night Susan walked into our Sunday evening service, which is a full gospel service. She found herself on the floor laughing for forty-five minutes straight. Three-quarters of an hour set her free from eighteen years of depression! Susan has now been with us nearly four years. She is one of the happiest and freest people I know. God set her free through laughter. There are many ways to kick-start your life of laughter. Of course the best way is to let God make you laugh. The second best is to laugh on purpose from an internal joy. Next is to stimulate laughter through an outside source.

How can you make laughter a part of your daily life? Here are five ideas I adapted from an article by psychologist Cindy Solliday-McRoy, PhD:[14]

1. Start with a smile. Forcing yourself to smile, even if you don't feel "happy," will trigger a "happy response" in your brain that can actually cause you to feel happier.[15]

2. Take a laugh break. Just as you might take a coffee break, take a few minutes each day to laugh. Read funny quotes or watch babies laughing on YouTube. Laughing will lift your spirits.

3. Maintain a sense of humor. Tell some jokes and don't take yourself too seriously. As you begin to see the humor in situations, you'll be able to find the silver lining in life and navigate more easily through difficult circumstances.[16]

4. Seek out fun and laughter. Don't wait for it to come to you. Watch funny movies and TV shows,

read comic strips, go to clean comedy clubs, or watch a comedian on YouTube. If you do, I'm sure you'll find something to laugh about.

5. Find a laughing buddy. We need one another not just to get the serious kingdom work done, but also to laugh and have fun together. We all need someone in our lives we can be silly with.

ANOINTED TO LAUGH

The Spirit of the Lord GOD is upon Me…to console those who mourn in Zion, to give them beauty for ashes, the oil of joy for mourning, the garment of praise for the spirit of heaviness.

—ISAIAH 61:1–3

God anointed Jesus with the Holy Spirit and power, enabling Him to go about doing good and healing all who were oppressed and in control of the devil (Acts 10:38). His anointing healed dullness, mourning, and heaviness. Jesus was smeared with the ability to remove discouragement, disappointment, and any other form of oppression.

The anointing makes freedom readily accessible and empowers *us* to give beauty for ashes, the oil of joy for mourning, and the garment of praise to take away heaviness. The Bible says that "where the Spirit of the Lord is, there is liberty" (2 Cor. 3:17). As long as the Holy Spirit is still in the earth, as long as He is still smearing His power and presence on people, He will give them beauty, the oil of joy, and the garments of praise.

With beauty, the Holy Spirit gives a glimmering headdress. This sounds like a crown (Isa. 28:5). God's presence gives you glory that is superior to any mental or emotional pain you might experience. He will restore your dignity and nobility, as He did for Sarah.

The oil of joy is also part of the consoling process of the Lord. It can be rubbed on to you on purpose. It can be messy, and it will drip if it is applied heavily. It can rub off onto others when you bump into them. It is transferable. You can receive and give joy at will, and it will handle all kinds of mourning and sorrow.

The garment of praise is worn, just like the crown of glory and the oil of joy. The garment of praise is to be wrapped around you, not only to remove heaviness, but also to prevent it.

You are God's child. Adorn your head with glory, smear yourself with joy, and wrap yourself with praise. Do this every day on purpose until the bright and shining morning star shines His light upon you. If it doesn't break the first day, put on your royal garment again. Do it again and again until you have reversed every hint of the curse and disappointment.

God Himself has made provision for you to live, love, and laugh. Life is good! God is good! Make up your mind that you were made to live in newness of life and spend every day purposefully celebrating His goodness.

NOTES

CHAPTER 2
FIND THE GOOD LIFE

1. Moshe Gans, *Success!* (N.p.: Art Scroll/Mesorah, 1976), 17.
2. Ibid.
3. *Thayer's Greek Lexicon,* PC Study Bible formatted Electronic Database (Seattle, WA: Biblesoft, 2006), s.v. "logizomai," (NT3049).
4. Oral Roberts, *Expect a Miracle* (Nashville: Thomas Nelson, 1998), 198.
5. Gans, *Success!*, 18.

CHAPTER 3
LOOK ON THE RIGHT SIDE

1. *Biblesoft's New Exhaustive Strong's Numbers and Concordance With Expanded Greek-Hebrew Dictionary,* CD-ROM (Seattle, WA: Biblesoft, Inc. and International Bible Translators, Inc., 1994, 2003, 2006), s.v. "shachar," (OT 7836).
2. *Brown-Driver-Briggs Hebrew and English Lexicon,* Unabridged, Electronic Database, (Seattle, WA: Biblesoft, Inc., 2006), (OT 7836).
3. *Thayer's Greek Lexicon,* s.v. "phroneo," (NT 5426).
4. *Blue Letter Bible,* Dictionaries, s.v. "abhor," https://www.blue letterbible.org/search/Dictionary/viewTopic.cfm?topic=IT0000035,KT 0000004,VT0000003 (accessed December 8, 2014).
5. *Roget's 21st Century Thesaurus, Third Edition* (Princeton, NJ: Philip Lief Group, 2009), s.v. "abhor," http://www.thesaurus.com/browse/abhor (accessed December 8, 2014).
6. Joyce Meyer, "The Truth About Prayer: What It Is and How It Works," *Christian Post,* July 6, 2012, http://www.christianpost.com/news/the-truth-about-prayer-what-it-is-and-how-it-works-77754/ (accessed December 8, 2014).

CHAPTER 4
AGREE WITH THE VOICE OF FAITH

1. Dictionary.com, s.v. "agree," http://dictionary.reference.com/
browse/agree?s=t (accessed October 14, 2014).
2. *Thayer's Greek Lexicon*, s.v. "suschematizo" (NT 4964).
3. Ibid., s.v. "metamorphoo" (NT 3339).
4. *How Do You Know?* directed by James L. Brooks (Los Angeles:
Columbia Pictures, 2011), DVD, http://www.imdb.com/title/tt1341188/
quotes (accessed October 14, 2014).

CHAPTER 5
MASTER URGES AND EXPECTATIONS

1. Vernon L. Allen, *Psychological Factors in Poverty* (Chicago:
Markham Publishing Company, 1970).
2. I highly recommend *Change Your Brain, Change Your Life* by
Daniel G. Amen for more on the subject.

CHAPTER 6
TAKE A LICKIN' AND KEEP ON TICKIN'

1. Dictionary.com, s.v. "circum," http://dictionary.reference.com
/browse/circum (accessed December 16, 2014).
2. *Biblesoft's New Exhaustive Strong's Numbers and Concordance
With Expanded Greek-Hebrew Dictionary*, s.v. "qavah," (OT 6960).
3. Nancy Douglas, "How Do Bald Eagles Learn to Fly?", eHow
.com, http://www.ehow.com/about_6503709_do-bald-eagles-learn-fly
_.html#ixzz2rpKt4Nma (accessed December 16, 2014).
4. *Biblesoft's New Exhaustive Strong's Numbers and Concordance
With Expanded Greek-Hebrew Dictionary*, s.v. "mashak" (OT 4900).
5. Ibid., s.v. "bow'" (OT 935).
6. Ibid., s.v. "ta'avah."
7. Dictionary.com, s.v., "longing," http://dictionary.reference.com/
browse/longing (accessed December 16, 2014).

CHAPTER 7
CHOOSE HAPPINESS

1. Napoleon Hill, *Outwitting the Devil* (New York: Sterling Publishing, 2011), 13.
2. *Biblesoft's New Exhaustive Strong's Numbers and Concordance
With Expanded Greek-Hebrew Dictionary*, s.v. "rasha'" (OT 7563).

3. Chabad.org, "Tehillim—Psalms—Chapter 1," http://www
.chabad.org/library/Bible_cdo/aid/16222#showrashi=true (accessed
December 16, 2014).

CHAPTER 8
NAVIGATING THE STORMS OF LIFE

1. *Thayer's Greek Lexicon*, PC Study Bible Formatted Electronic s.v.
"echo" (NT 2192).
2. Dictionary.com, s.v., "conscience," http://dictionary.reference
.com/browse/conscience (accessed December 17, 2014).

CHAPTER 9
I CAN CHANGE IT

1. *Biblesoft's New Exhaustive Strong's Numbers and Concordance
With Expanded Greek-Hebrew Dictionary*, s.v. "energeo" (NT 1754).
2. Ibid., s.v. "prostithemi," (NT 4369).

CHAPTER 10
IT'S ABOUT TIME

1. *Biblesoft's New Exhaustive Strong's Numbers and Concordance
With Expanded Greek-Hebrew Dictionary*, s.v. "horaios" (NT 5611).
2. Ibid., s.v. "megas," (NT 3173).
3. Ibid., s.v. "energes," (NT 1756).
4. Biblestudytools.com, s.v. "skandalon," http://www.biblestudy
tools.com/lexicons/greek/nas/skandalon.html (accessed December 21,
2014).
5. Ibid., s.v. "anagke" (NT 318), http://www.biblestudytools.com/
lexicons/greek/nas/anagke.html (accessed December 21, 2014).

CHAPTER 11
THAT'S RIDICULOUS

1. Webster's Dictionary 1828, s.v. "derision," http://websters
dictionary1828.com/ (accessed December 21, 2014).
2. Ibid., s.v. "ridicule."
3. *Biblesoft's New Exhaustive Strong's Numbers and Concordance
With Expanded Greek-Hebrew Dictionary*, s.v. "yad" (OT 3027).

CHAPTER 12
IT'S TOO HARD

1. BibleStudyTools.com, s.v. "pala,'" (OT 6381), http://www
.biblestudytools.com/lexicons/hebrew/nas/pala.html (accessed
December 21, 2014).
2. Dictionary.com, s.v. "discern," http://dictionary.reference.com/
browse/discern (accessed December 21, 2014).

CHAPTER 13
HONEST TO GOD

1. Dictionary.com, s.v., "disappoint," http://dictionary.reference
.com/browse/disappoint (accessed December 21, 2014).
2. *Biblesoft's New Exhaustive Strong's Numbers and Concordance
With Expanded Greek-Hebrew Dictionary*, s.v. "kachash" (OT 3584).
3. Dictionary.com, s.v., "honest-to-goodness" http://dictionary
.reference.com/browse/honest to goodness (accessed December 21,
2014).

CHAPTER 14
I AM EXPECTING A VISITOR

1. Blue Letter Bible, Hebrew Lexicon, s.v. "emeth," (H571 KJV),
http://www.blueletterbible.org/lang/lexicon/lexicon.cfm?Strongs
=H571&t=KJV (accessed December 21, 2014).
2. BibleStudyTools.com, s.v. "helikia," http://www.biblestudytools
.com/lexicons/greek/nas/helikia.html (accessed February 2, 2015).

CHAPTER 15
FULLNESS OF JOY

1. *Thayer's Greek Lexicon*, s.v. "lambanó" (NT 2983).
2. Ibid., s.v. "dunamis," (NT 1411).
3. Ibid., s.v. "hegeomai," (NT 2233).
4. *Brown-Driver-Briggs Hebrew and English Lexicon*, s.v.
"mishmar," (OT 4929).
5. Blue Letter Bible, Hebrew Lexicon, s.v., "těruw`ah," (H8643),
https://www.blueletterbible.org/lang/lexicon/lexicon.cfm?strongs
=H8643 (accessed December 21, 2014).

CHAPTER 16
GOD MADE ME LAUGH

1. Brainyquote.com, "Mark Twain Quotes," http://www.brainy quote.com/quotes/quotes/m/marktwain125786.html (accessed December 21, 2014).

2. Berit Brogaard, "Effects of Laughter on the Human Brain," Livestrong.com, March 11, 2014, http://www.livestrong.com/article/ 158238-the-effects-of-laughter-on-the-human-brain/ (accessed December 21, 2014).

3. MNT, "The Benefits of 'Mirthful Laughter,' Coupled With Standard Diabetic Treatment," April 17, 2009, http://www.medicalnews today.com/releases/146449.php (accessed December 21, 2014).

4. Ibid.

5. Forquestions.com, "Benefits From Laughing Out Loud," http:// forquestions.com/benefits-from-laughing-out-loud/141 (accessed January 22, 2015).

6. Jeanette Pavini, "How to Fit Fitness Into What You Already Do Every Day," Huffpost Healthy Living, http://www.huffingtonpost.com/ jeanette-pavini/health-and-fitness_b_5660223.html (accessed January 23, 2015).

7. Melanie Rudolph, "Laughter Yoga Worldwide News Flash: LiveSTRONG Website," Laughter Yoga University, April 23, 2013, http://www.laughteryoga.org/english/blog/blog_detail/441 (accessed December 21, 2014).

8. Laughter Yoga, "The Effects of Laughter on the Human Brain," http://laughteryoga.org/english/laughteryoga/details/201 (accessed December 21, 2014).

9. Enda Junkins, "Role of Laughter in Psychotherapy," http://www .laughtertherapy.com/enda-junkins (accessed December 21, 2014).

10. Cancer Treament Centers of America, "Laughter Therapy," http://www.cancercenter.com/treatments/laughter-therapy/ (accessed December 21, 2014); American Cancer Society, "Humor Therapy," http://www.cancer.org/treatment/treatmentsandsideeffects/ complementaryandalternativemedicine/mindbodyandspirit/humor -therapy (accessed December 21, 2014).

11. Daniel Lapin and Susan Lapin, *Buried Treasure: Secrets for Living From the Lord's Language* (Mercer Island, WA: Lifecodex Publishing, LLC, 2012), 45.

12. Rabbi Nosson Scherman, *The Chumash: The Torah, Haftaros and Five Megillos With a Commentary Anthologized From the Rabbinic Writings* (Brooklyn, NY: Mesorah Publications, 1998), 97.

13. Laughter Yoga Switzerland, "Childlike Playfulness," http://www.laughteryogaswitzerland.com/#!services/galleryPage (accessed December 21, 2014).

14. The article "5 Ways to De-Stress, In-Joy and Laugh It Off!" by Dr. Cindy Solliday-McRoy is no longer accessible at Livestrong.com.

15. Alex Korb, "Smile: A Powerful Tool," PsychologyToday.com, July 31, 2012, http://www.psychologytoday.com/blog/prefrontal-nudity/201207/smile-powerful-tool (accessed January 23, 2015).

16. Mike Robins, "Don't Take Yourself Too Seriously," HuffPost Healthy Living, June 25, 2015, http://www.huffingtonpost.com/mike-robbins/dont-take-yourself-too-se_b_5213643.html (accessed January 23, 2015).

EMPOWERED
TO RADICALLY CHANGE
YOUR WORLD